Behind the Veil

One Man's Journey from Opioid Addiction to Spirituality and Beyond

What People Are Saying About

Behind the Veil

Behind the Veil takes the reader on a journey of life choices; some good, some bad, but all of which lead to enlightenment. The early chapters detail the decisions Tim Malone initially wished he did not make. However, he ultimately realizes that those choices led him to experience unconditional love from a special dog named Boo Boo. This unexpected relationship helped Tim find his way back into the light of life. *Behind the Veil* then takes the reader from the moment Tim begins his spiritual journey to all that he has encountered and learned about spirit guides, angels, orbs, the afterlife, and so much more. I loved how Tim recorded his journey for the reader. It is a spellbinding book that will captivate any reader, no matter what stage of their own personal journey they are at. Plus, there are so many tips, suggestions and advice that we can all benefit from. An enlightening read!
Kathy Crosswell, coauthor of *Enlightenment Through Orbs: The Awesome Truth Revealed, Ascension Through Orbs* and *The Keys to the Universe: Access the Ancient Secrets by Attuning to the Power and Wisdom of the Cosmos*

Tim Malone takes us on a deeply personal journey in *Behind the Veil,* from his stumble into the darkness of opioid addiction to the heights of spiritual awakening. His journey is one of discovery, sparked by his dog Boo Boo, reminding us that spiritual growth can begin in the most unexpected ways. This deeply personal account, filled with profound insights on meditation, manifestation, and connecting with spirit guides,

serves as both a memoir and a guidebook for those seeking their own path to enlightenment.
Jake Zortman, producer, director, cinematographer, and author of *The Rise of the Legends*

This book has many layers — an introspective personal journey, the healing power of LOVE, and an opening to realms beyond this physical level. A great read.
Miriam Goldstein, Minister in the Church of the Movement of Spiritual Inner Awareness

A delightful, touching account of a profound redemption, of a journey into and out of the devastating world of opioids. Malone's journey is inspiring. He demonstrates not only how easily we can fall, but also gives immense hope to those who seek to emerge from the depths — Malone doesn't just try to return to the good life of once a time ago. He pushes far further, grappling with the heights of human purpose, consciousness, and existence.
Dr. Saqib Qureshi, best-selling author of *Reconstructing Strategy, The Broken Contract,* and *Being Muslim Today*

Behind the Veil

One Man's Journey from Opioid Addiction to Spirituality and Beyond

Tim Malone
Jessica Franzini

BOOKS
London, UK
Washington, DC, USA

First published by O-Books, 2025
O-Books is an imprint of Collective Ink Ltd.,
Unit 11, Shepperton House, 89 Shepperton Road, London, N1 3DF
office@collectiveinkbooks.com
www.collectiveinkbooks.com
www.o-books.com

For distributor details and how to order, please visit the 'Ordering' section on our website.

ISBN: 978 1 80341 936 7
978 1 80341 946 6 (ebook)
Library of Congress Control Number: 2024944677

A CIP catalogue record for this book is available from the British Library.

Design: Lapiz Digital Services

UK: Printed and bound by CPI Group (UK) Ltd, Croydon, CR0 4YY
Printed in North America by CPI GPS partners

The author of this book does not dispense medical advice or prescribe the use of any technique as a form of treatment for physical, emotional, or medical problems without the advice of a physician, either directly or indirectly. The intent of the author is only to offer information of a general nature to help you in your quest for emotional and spiritual well-being. In the event you use any of the information in this book for yourself, which is your constitutional right, the author and the publisher assume no responsibility for your actions.

Contents

To my beloved wife, Denise, and my wonderful daughters, Tori, Lauren, and Paige, your patience and unwavering support have made this journey possible. With all my love, I also dedicate this book to Boo Boo, who went above and beyond what any dog could do. Not only did Boo Boo save me from addiction, but also guided me to the most beautiful and sacred places, where the Holy Ones stand in line to help, assist, and love me. All of your love has been more than I ever could have imagined. Thank you for being my guiding light.

– Tim

To my husband, Lou, and son, Sam, who inspire me daily. To my Dad, who has provided for me in every conceivable way. To my "Boo Boo," Charlie, who has brought immeasurable joy to our family and literally changed the trajectory of my life. But I dedicate this book especially to my Mom, for in addition to being my greatest cheerleader, it is her gift of writing that I have so luckily inherited.

– Jessica

Acknowledgements

I am deeply grateful to all the souls who have guided me on this journey of spiritual discovery and growth.

My wife, Denise, holds a special place of distinction for all the reasons I described within these pages. However, one book is simply not enough to mention all the ways in which Denise has been my greatest source of support. I thank you each and every day for continuing to love me.

To my daughters and stepsons, Tori, Paige, Lauren, Beau, and Tyler, I hold much appreciation for trusting me in what I was saying was true, even when it seemed beyond strange.

My heartfelt thanks to my first spiritual mentor, Cheryl Gentry. I am also grateful to Rhonda Etherton, a wonderful teacher, and to Shera Herndon and Jennifer Williams in our meditation group. We spent countless hours delving into the divine, and if you didn't know it before, please know now that our discussions after meditations were so instrumental in my growth.

Special thanks go to the Earth and Spirit Center and its director, Kyle Kramer, along with Tim Darst, director for Earth Literacy. The Earth and Spirit Center, with its 27 acres of pristine woodlands, is where I found the Healing Mary statue. It was also at an Earth and Spirit Center event that I met my dear friends, Tom and Di Kerrigan, who have helped and guided me in numerous ways along my journey. The Louisville Presbyterian Seminary's new president, Andrew Pomerville, graciously allowed me access to the beautiful Caldwell Chapel whenever I needed it. This chapel has become my own sacred temple to meditate and communicate with the Holy Ones. I thank you so much for providing me this incredible, beautiful, and inspirational space. I appreciate this gift more than words can express.

I have so much appreciation and love for my assistant, Dominique Pendergrass, my first true believer, who has grown to become quite the mystic himself in a very short period. This project would not have happened without Dominique. Thank you to the incredibly talented Ryan Daly, now a close associate, who is working on a documentary to complement *Behind the Veil*. Ryan, Dominique, and I have traveled several states, meeting people to document their stories, and have spent countless hours in my backyard, trying new techniques to capture better pictures and clarity.

When it came time to find a writer for the book, Dominique found two writers who didn't work out for various reasons. It was divine destiny that Jessica Franzini took the assignment. She believed in my story from the beginning and supported the truth, no matter how unusual it seemed. Jessica's work ethic was beyond impressive, and she was able to turn my verbal ramblings into a masterpiece of new-age writing. She holds a special place in my heart.

To the cast of divine Holy Ones, thank you for delivering me from addiction, carefully plotting and planning my path to enlightenment, and continuing to amaze me with your images, words, and directions. My spirit guides, especially Carol, my seraphim guardians, Soss and Otta, my hierophants, Tula and Siphix, the wonderful midway creatures, and various other celestial visitors who have visited my backyard portal: I thank you all. Mere words cannot adequately express the magnitude of my love and appreciation.

To you, the reader, I find it hard to put into words my appreciation for buying and reading our book. I hope it helps souls find their way in this crazy, beautiful, exciting, inspirational world we live in. Remember, love is the currency behind the veil.

Finally, to my Boo Boo ... if it were not for you, I would not be on this path. I think of you and am loving you every single day.

With heartfelt gratitude, Tim

There are so many people to thank for their support during this journey! First and foremost, the man who gave me this incredible opportunity, Tim Malone. Tim and I met less than a year ago but we had an immediate and very real connection. Tim, it has been a genuine honor to work with you to share what you have learned on your journey. I thank you for the great collaborative energy and all of the kudos along the way. My life is better for having met you. Thank you.

I want to thank my husband, Lou, who sacrificed our time together so I could write day and night. This meant fewer date nights and more take-out meals, along with him taking on extra household chores. He did all this without a single complaint and was always there to support and cheer me on. As a fellow writer, he also played a crucial role as my editor, dedicating many late nights to helping me perfect my work.

My son Sam, also a professional writer, sent his encouragement from Washington DC, always ready to celebrate each of my achievements. I'm also incredibly grateful to my mom, dad, sister Adria, my brothers David and Adam, my brother-in-law Alan, and sisters-in-law Paula, Diane, and Raquel for their unwavering support and timely high-five emojis whenever I reached a new milestone. A special shout out to Dominique Pendergrass. He may be Tim's assistant, but he helped me numerous times throughout the year while working on this project and even after. He is immensely talented and has a heart of gold and his assistance has been invaluable.

There is one person who has been my guiding light in my spiritual education and that is my Aunt Miriam. Throughout my life, Miriam has been my "go-to" person for all things unseen or unknown (yet). She has helped me to question what is important in this life and opened my mind to what is possible in this world and beyond. Without Miriam, there is no *Behind the Veil*.

A heartfelt thank you to all my friends, both old and new, who have been there for me. A special mention to my friends Joann and Bill Lorson who have been my extraordinary teachers in how to live every day with genuine gratitude; and to Robert Scott and Koen Delaere, who were especially supportive as I finished *Behind the Veil*, often stepping in with support and meals when I was too busy to cook.

Thank you all. I am truly grateful.

Jessica

It's Just a Dog

by Richard Biby

From time to time, people tell me, "lighten up, it's just a dog," or,
"that's a lot of money for just a dog."
They don't understand the distance traveled, the time spent,
or the costs involved for "just a dog."
Some of my proudest moments have come about with "just a dog."
Many hours have passed and my only company was "just a dog,"
but I did not once feel slighted.
Some of my saddest moments have been brought about by "just a dog,"
and in those days of darkness, the gentle touch of "just a dog"
gave me comfort and reason to overcome the day.
If you, too, think it's "just a dog,"
then you will probably understand phrases like
"just a friend,"
"just a sunrise,"
or "just a promise."
"Just a dog" brings into my life the very essence of friendship,
trust, and pure unbridled joy.
"Just a dog" brings out the compassion and patience
that make me a better person.
Because of "just a dog," I will rise early, take long walks
and look longingly to the future.
So, for me and folks like me, it's not "just a dog"
but an embodiment of all the hopes and dreams of the future,
the fond memories of the past,
and the pure joy of the moment.
"Just a dog" brings out what's good in me
and diverts my thoughts away from myself and the worries of the day.
I hope that someday they can understand that it's not "just a dog,"
but the thing that gives me humanity and keeps me from being "just
a man or woman." So, the next time you hear the phrase "just a dog,"
just smile ... because they "just don't understand."

Chapter 1

On the Rocks

The two most important days in your life are the day you are born and the day you figure out why.

Mark Twain

Reflecting on my childhood in Louisville, vibrant memories, poignant losses, and transformative experiences emerge, painting a picture of a life richly lived despite its complexities. The innocence of my youth intertwined with the stark realities of my family upheaval. My life was a crucible of experiences that forged the person I have become, a narrative interwoven with the joys of discovery, the pain of loss, and the power of resilience. In this journey through the highs and lows of childhood and into the intricacies of family life, I learned invaluable lessons about love, loss, redemption, and the indomitable spirit of perseverance, shaping not just my memories but the essence of my being.

Young Tim Malone

Growing up in the Highlands neighborhood, my life was imbued with a blend of cherished boyhood adventures and complex family dynamics. Born in 1959, I was reared in a middle-class neighborhood, where playing football and the innocence of youth often intersected with more profound, challenging experiences.

My father, a foreman at a cigarette company, and my mother, a stay-at-home mom, were young parents, both 22 when they had me. I have three brothers: Chris, who is two years my senior, and Terry and Ted, my younger twin brothers, also by two years. A stranger wouldn't even assume that Terry and Ted are brothers, let alone twins, as they look nothing alike.

My childhood in the late'60s and early'70s was marked by freedom and exploration. I participated in a swim club, played football, and had many friends. A ball field across the street served as my playground, and solo bus rides to the movies from the fourth grade on fostered my independence. A nearby quarry was the site of many adventures with my brothers and friends, as was an old spring-fed pool at St. Agnes Church. We would sneak in there and go skinny dipping. When I think about those times now, it is remarkable because the pool was close to a significant discovery I made later in life, as described in Chapter 3. It is just astonishing that it took another 45 years to uncover the treasure that I do, but I now realize that I discovered it at a time in my life when I needed it most.

In 1969, my father left his job to buy and run a head-hunting business, a bold move at a time when temporary jobs weren't typical. His venture into placing professionals in permanent positions marked a new chapter for our family. However, our family's harmony (or what I thought was harmonious) was disrupted when my father's infidelity came to light, a reality I was soon after uncomfortably made aware of, even as a child.

The revelation of his transgressions deeply affected our family, leading to a pivotal moment orchestrated by my mother. To confront the reality of his actions, she drove my brothers and me to his mistress's house, leaving us at the end of a strange street to face the harsh truth of our father's betrayal. I am not sure what her intention was; I am not sure she even knew, for she turned the car around a half-hour later and picked us back up. It was too late, though. The memory of the experience is etched in my psyche all these years later. I will never forget sitting on the sidewalk outside a house I didn't know and being told my father was in there with another woman. It was a jolt in every conceivable way.

Ultimately, my parents divorced, beginning a turbulent chapter in our lives. My father disappeared and began his transformative journey for himself. It became clear that this journey did not include his sons. My mother, demonstrating her resilience, became our sole parent. We had a complicated relationship with our mother. However, I thank her today for fostering our independence while still being present for memorable special moments, like taking us to rock concerts.

My father soon remarried to a woman named Betty, who we all genuinely liked. After that, he returned to my life as if he never left. He became involved with everything I did, including attending every football game and eventually becoming the team's coach. We won the state championship, and I was chosen to be on the All-State team. If my father was trying to make up for lost time, he succeeded. He also became a regular at church, which signaled a dramatic change. However, the catalyst for this remains a mystery to me.

Another significant part of my childhood was my relationship with my grandmother. I cherished her deeply and was grief-stricken when she died. I was only eight years old, but she had a lasting impact on me. Her genuine love and understanding provided a profound connection, illustrating how time does not measure the depth of relationships.

I have always passionately loved and shown affection for animals, sparking my first dream of becoming a veterinarian. I loved Basset Hounds in particular and always had them growing up. However, Bassets can easily get distracted by interesting scents. Because of their nose, Basset Hounds tend to wander, continually creating perilous situations. I was finding myself in a recurring pattern of love and loss due to their instincts, and it was agonizing. When I lost my beloved Basset named Floyd in my first marriage, I never wanted to have another dog again. My career path veered from veterinary science, but my love for animals remained.

College Life

After graduating high school, I embarked on my college journey at Eastern Kentucky University, an hour and a half away from my family home. It was 1977 when dorm roommate pairings were more a roll of the dice than a meticulously matched process based on shared interests. Despite this lack of precision, fortune smiled upon me, and I found myself sharing a room with someone who would become my best friend throughout my college years.

Later in life, when I delved into personal assessments by taking the Myers-Briggs test, I discovered insights about my aptitudes and interests. These evaluations revealed that my strengths lay in sales and marketing — a field where I eventually found my professional footing. This realization was a moment of clarity, aligning my inherent skills with my career.

College life, in all, was vibrant and fulfilling. I joined a fraternity, immersed myself in the social scene, and enjoyed the company of numerous friends and girlfriends, particularly cherishing a relationship with an incredible girlfriend during my freshman and sophomore years. I also had a great job at a local pizza joint. These experiences, rich in camaraderie and adventure, were the cornerstone of my college years, leaving me with a trove of memories I wouldn't trade for anything.

Early Career

I graduated with a degree in marketing, a field I felt drawn to and excited about. Almost immediately after college, life took a significant turn. I reconnected with a special girl from Louisville and our relationship quickly escalated, especially when we discovered she was pregnant. This led quickly to marriage, marking the start of a new chapter in my life that was as unexpected as it was transformative.

I entered the world of employment and family life almost simultaneously. My first job took me to Lexington, Kentucky, where I started working for Sherwin-Williams. It was 1982, and my annual salary was $13,000. It was a challenging economic period due to soaring interest rates that stifled construction and paint sales.

However, I spotted an opportunity in the market that Sherwin-Williams had yet to capitalize on – carpet sales. At the time, there was a boom in apartment construction, and carpets were in high demand. I pivoted to selling carpets, which propelled me to become the top salesman in the United States for Sherwin-Williams, earning numerous accolades for my performance.

My success was garnering a lot of attention, and before long, I was offered a position as a district manager at Congoleum Flooring. This was a clear step up in my career. I worked there until the early '90s, when the entrepreneurial itch led me to venture into my own business. Meanwhile, my father ran a small staffing company. Despite my achievements and desire to join him, he believed I needed more experience.

Determined to prove my mettle, I started a business with partners, which performed exceptionally well, but I was still living in Louisville and the daily commute to Lexington was taxing. Eventually, I joined my father's company, convinced I could make a significant impact. I confidently stepped in despite his reservations and concerns about the financial implications.

Within three months, I secured a major account. This achievement brought in millions and underscored my ability to thrive in challenging situations. This accomplishment boosted the business and reinforced my belief in my capabilities and the value of perseverance and hard work.

In the staffing business, our primary service revolves around providing companies with a flexible workforce, especially during peak seasons, like Christmas, or when their production demands increase. For example, a company might want to hire a hundred temporary workers for a period, like three months, to handle the extra workload. This flexibility allowed them to scale their labor force up or down based on their immediate needs without committing to long-term employment contracts.

Over time, these companies realized they could use this temporary workforce as a recruitment pool. Instead of going through the traditional hiring process, they would observe the temps in action and offer permanent positions to the standout performers. This approach not only streamlined their hiring process but also contributed to the broader success of American businesses by enabling them to adapt quickly to market demands.

While the staffing business flourished, I found the direct hire aspect needed to be more varied. My passion lay in the dynamic, ever-changing nature of staffing, which allowed me to build and maintain numerous valuable relationships in the industry.

My Girls

My marriage brought us three wonderful daughters: Tori, Lauren, and Paige. This new chapter in my life was filled with a constant buzz of activities, ranging from tennis matches to dance recitals, shaping our family's routine and bonding us in unique ways.

Our home became a lively place where the sound of sports and music mingled with the everyday chaos of family life. Despite our financial situation, we made sure that our daughters' interests and activities were a top priority, creating a vibrant and active home environment where their passions could thrive.

With her steadfast dedication, my wife was the pillar of this dynamic. She put the needs and ambitions of our daughters above everything, often sacrificing her interests to support their endeavors. Her commitment meant that Tori, Paige, and Lauren always felt prioritized and loved, with someone in their corner cheering them on, no matter the circumstance.

As a father, I took pride in watching our daughters grow and develop, their characters shaped by the array of experiences and the nurturing environment at home. This phase of our lives, marked by its simplicity and dedication to family, taught us all valuable lessons about priorities, support, and the enduring strength of family ties. Our daughters' interests didn't just help them grow; they brought us all closer, creating a family dynamic where everyone's journey was integral to our collective story.

During our 18 years of marriage, however, the imbalance of my wife prioritizing our daughters over me and my needs began to weigh on me. I sensed a void, as I was constantly being relegated to a lower tier in the family hierarchy, below the kids and her extended family. I was clearly at the bottom of her pyramid of importance. This led to a profound sense of loneliness and disconnection, contributing to my infidelity – an action I deeply regret and have since come to understand more about.

The consequence of these challenging times was my difficult decision to leave my family. In this tumultuous period, I wrestled with various emotions: the guilt over parting ways with my wife, the pain of knowing my daughters might feel deserted, and my battle to find stability in a life that seemed to be coming apart at the seams. I sought help from my therapist, Fred, to work through this storm of feelings. However, despite Fred's efforts to guide me, I wasn't fully addressing the extent of my turmoil. Instead, I found a misguided comfort in substances like Valium, as it seemed to help with the overwhelming distress.

Despite the chaos of my personal life, my business continued to run, largely thanks to my brother and our partnership. He was deeply involved in the operations, and we had a team of competent employees who expertly managed the business. It is because of my brother and our staff that our company not only survived my addiction but thrived.

Looking back on that time, I don't know how I survived. Even with the challenges before them, though ... challenges that I am responsible for creating ... all of my daughters have built beautiful lives for themselves, and I am a proud grandfather to their children. Today, our family connection is strong, and we share many experiences, like birthday parties and holidays, traveling, attending concerts, spending time at our lake house, and just hanging out on Sunday afternoons. Although our family has changed, especially with the divorce, we have a sense of unity and closeness.

My ex-wife has found a fulfilling path following our separation. She has since remarried and resides in Lake Forest. Her career involves visiting doctors' offices, where she represents a company selling braces and physical therapy equipment — a role she excels in and finds rewarding.

Despite the years since our divorce, our relationship remains amicable, with occasional playful jabs adding humor to our interactions. Knowing we can communicate openly and maintain a positive connection is reassuring, demonstrating a mature approach to our post-marital relationship. I get along with Denise's ex-husband as well. I recently arranged for him, his son, and her sons to join us on a trip to Wisconsin. Our commitment to maintaining these positive connections is a conscious effort to foster a sense of unity and understanding for our "modern family."

Reflecting on the lessons I've learned from my children; I realize how profoundly they've influenced my perspective on life and parenting. My daughters display an exceptional dedication to their children, investing time and energy in various activities to ensure their well-rounded development. This commitment has made me appreciate the value of being present and actively involved in my children's lives, whether by supporting their tennis tournaments or simply being there for them on a daily basis.

Paige, my youngest, mirrors aspects of my personality, such as ambition and a tendency toward impatience and stress. Her approach to challenges, marked by a drive to excel and a harsh self-criticism when things don't go as planned, has made me introspect my reactions to adversity. Observing her, I've learned the importance of self-compassion and the need to ease the pressure we place on ourselves.

My children's love and the unique lessons they've imparted, often without even realizing it, have been invaluable. They've shown me different facets of life, helped me grow as a person, and underscored the reciprocal nature of learning between parent and child. Each day with them brings new insights, reminding me that while I may be their teacher in some respects, they are equally my guides in my life's journey.

Denise

I met Denise in 2000. At that time, she was an HR coordinator for Circuit City in Marion, Illinois. I had to visit their new warehouse, and that is where we met and started working closely together.

Emerging from the shadows of our past failed marriages, Denise and I discovered a connection that quickly deepened, revealing a magnetic pull between us. As we peeled back the layers of each other's lives, our mutual attraction was undeniable, blossoming into a romance that defied the miles separating us.

I lived in Louisville, Kentucky, while Denise called Marion, Illinois, her home, a three and a half hour drive away. But as they say, love knows no bounds, and we were determined to bridge the gap. Weekends became our sanctuary, a time to collapse the distance and immerse ourselves in each other's company.

With her vibrant spirit, Denise brought a lightness and depth to my life that was utterly refreshing. Her strength was palpable, a trait that resonated deeply with me, given our shared experiences of navigating life after unsuccessful marriages. Her sense of humor often caught me off-guard, bringing laughter and joy into moments that might have otherwise been tinged with the residue of our pasts. She was not just fun but an adventure in human form, a constant reminder of the joy in everyday moments.

Her intellect was undeniable, drawing me in with conversations that ranged from the trivial to the profound. Denise had a unique way of looking at the world, a perspective that challenged and intrigued me equally. Together, we found a kind of partnership that was as enriching as it was comforting, a testament to the beauty of finding someone who complements and challenges you at the same time.

Despite the logistical hurdles of our long-distance romance, the foundation we were building was solid, anchored in mutual respect, deep affection, and an unwavering commitment to making each moment count.

During a trip to Aruba, I proposed, and luckily for me, Denise said, "Yes!"

We decided to get married on July 7, 2002, in a ceremony at my house. In hindsight, I sometimes feel that I missed an opportunity to spend time alone, to understand and rebuild myself before committing to another person. I recognize, though, that meeting and falling in love with Denise was a necessary chapter in my life, for that exact moment was when I most needed her offering of support and stability.

The end of my first marriage and the beginning of my new one with Denise marked a stark contrast. Our relationship was built on mutual respect and love, and a shared priority for each other's happiness and well-being. In over two decades with Denise, my commitment remains unwavering, with no distractions or missteps, proving to myself that past behaviors don't have to define or dictate future actions. This new partnership, where I feel valued and loved, taught me the significance of feeling equally important in a relationship, reshaping my understanding of love and partnership. I was at the top of Denise's pyramid.

Our new life together, however, was not without its challenges. After our honeymoon in Antigua, Denise and her two sons moved to Louisville. With my three girls and her two boys, the beginning of our journey was tumultuous. This reality and the fact that I was still emotionally untangling myself from the remnants of my first marriage did nothing to curb my budding addiction. Quite the opposite.

The chaos in my new family led me to seek solace in alcohol in addition to drugs. The path of self-destruction was in full swing. My therapist cautioned me about the risk of falling deeper into addiction during such a tumultuous period. Yet, despite these warnings, I found myself spiraling further, convincing myself and others that I was managing just fine.

As my addiction progressed, Denise was incredibly supportive, even though she wasn't fully aware of the extent of my problem. She was there for me through everything, providing unwavering support, never critical of the issues I was facing, the weight I was gaining, or the unusual hours I was keeping. Luckily, our marriage remained strong despite these difficulties and the everyday challenges of blending a family with children from previous relationships.

Descent into Addiction

What started with Valium expanded into a broader experimentation with various substances, culminating in what can only be described as a profound dependency.

The ensuing years are a blur of doctor visits, manipulated medical records, and a growing proficiency in acquiring and consuming hydrocodone.

It's essential to note that my therapist, who played a pivotal role in my mental health at the time, was not the one who prescribed these opioids. Furthermore, it is my opinion that the lax prescription practices of the early 2000s facilitated my descent into addiction. During that period, it was alarmingly easy to obtain opioid prescriptions like hydrocodone and Percocet from local doctors, as there was no interconnected system to track prescriptions across states.

Driven by my addiction's overpowering grip, I amassed around 900 pills at one point, traveling to different states and using falsified medical documents to procure these medications. For about $300 to $350, I could get a bottle of 90 pills with two legitimate refills, taking advantage of the pharmacies linked to these lenient doctors.

This addiction overshadowed my daily life. I consumed Ambien at night along with 14 hydrocodone pills, a dangerous cocktail that brought me close to death on several occasions. I often questioned the reality of my situation, struggling to comprehend how my life had spiraled to this point.

When rules and procedures started becoming more restrictive, my desperation drove me to extreme lengths. One time, I traveled to Florida to see a doctor known for easily prescribing pills. It was a reckless move, but I simply didn't care. Another moment that stands out was during a routine checkup when I learned I was 250 pounds, pre-diabetic, and had elevated liver enzymes — a consequence of the excessive Tylenol mixed with the hydrocodone I was consuming. Each pill contained not just the opioid but also a significant amount of Tylenol, which was wreaking havoc on my body.

To make matters worse, I was combining hydrocodone with Ambien to sleep, unaware of the deadly risk of this mix. I experienced a recurring nightmare where I was climbing a hill and never returning, a haunting vision that still lingers with me today. My mornings began with a Mike's Hard Lemonade and a couple of hydrocodone pills on my way to work. By the end of the day, it was safe to say that I had consumed more than 13 pills. I would actually lose count. This pattern was unsustainable, and these moments were clear signals that my life was spiraling out of control.

Chapter 2

I Don't Want a Dog

Dogs do speak, but only to those who know how to listen.
Orhan Pamuk

In 2007, I found myself grappling with the toughest phase of my addiction. During this challenging period, amidst the storm of my personal struggles, Denise made a decision that would unexpectedly shift the course of our lives. She walked through the door one day with a look of determined excitement and announced she had bought a Shih Tzu puppy.

This announcement took me aback since in the past I had made it abundantly clear that I never wanted a dog in our house. I had dogs before. I loved dogs before. Heck, I wanted to take care of dogs as a veterinarian. But I lost dogs before. I knew the work involved and the heartache they can bring, and in my current state of addiction, a dog was the last thing I thought I needed. "I don't want a dog!" I often had to make crystal clear.

At that point in my life, my addiction had me firmly in its grip. Remember, I was consuming a staggering 14 hydrocodone pills each day, an amount that now sends shivers down my spine just thinking about it. Physically, I was in terrible shape, a shadow of my former self, and mentally, I felt utterly lost. I was battling not just with the physical effects of the drugs but also with a crippling sense of despair and disconnection from everything that had once brought joy to my life. Denise, with her unwavering strength and optimism, seemed to see something beyond my addiction and my protests. She saw a chance for healing, for bringing a spark of something pure and joyful into our lives that was desperately needed. As it turns out, she was right.

Boo Boo

When the day came that the puppy was finally delivered to our home, a tiny, wriggling bundle of joy, it felt like a new chapter was beginning in our lives. I remember standing there, a bit bewildered but also curiously amused, as Denise held the little fur ball in her arms. I said to her, "Well since you went ahead and got the dog, I think it's only fair that I get to name her. So, we're gonna call her Boo Boo." The name came from my dad's second wife's son. He had a daughter who they affectionately called Boo Boo. I always thought that was a cute name, so I went with that.

It's funny how a small furry creature can have such a profound impact on a person. As much as the pets I had before taught me about unconditional love and the magic of animals, Boo Boo was somehow different. In the early days of her life with us, I had not yet fully anticipated just how different, nor the emotional connection that was about to develop.

Over time, as I started to engage more with Boo Boo, I began to see her as so much more than just a pet. I watched her unique personality unfold — her playful antics, her loving nudges, and the way she would tilt her head inquisitively when I talked to her. She became a companion, a source of joy and comfort, and an integral part of my daily life.

This shift in my perception didn't happen overnight. When she arrived, I still clung to my reluctance about having a dog. Denise explained right away that Boo Boo would need plenty of exercise, precisely long walks at least twice a day, and she thought it would be good for me to be the one to take her. So, I begrudgingly started to walk her around our neighborhood. At first, these walks felt like just another chore on my list, something I had to do rather than wanted to do. It took about a week of this new routine for me to start understanding the beauty of our growing companionship.

I remember vividly the exact moment that changed everything. I was sitting in the living room, lost in a book, enjoying a quiet afternoon. Out of the corner of my eye, I noticed Boo Boo quietly padding over to me. She settled beside my chair, and then with a gentle nudge, she lifted her paw and swiped at my leg, asking for attention. I looked down, and what I saw took my breath away. There she was, gazing up at me with these big, beautiful black eyes that emanated pure love and trust. In that singular, heartwarming moment, something inside me shifted. The walls I had built around my heart that told me I didn't need or want another dog began to crumble.

It's hard to describe, but it felt like I was being hit right in the heart with a dart. Suddenly, all of my reservations, all of my hesitations about having Boo Boo in my life, seemed so trivial compared to the bond that was forming between us. My life was forever changed, literally. The daily walks became something I looked forward to, a time for reflection, connection, and appreciation of the simple joys of life.

Having Boo Boo depending and relying on me for her care was an experience that profoundly affected me. Every time I looked into her eyes, seeing that innocence and vulnerability stirred something deep within me, often bringing tears to my eyes. It's a feeling that still overwhelms me with emotion, even now, as I sit and reminisce about our time together. When it comes to Boo Boo, words often feel inadequate. A level of emotion is hard to capture in mere sentences.

I've realized, primarily through sharing my story with others, that every pet lover understands this indescribable bond. It's a connection that goes beyond words, beyond the usual forms of affection we're familiar with. When people ask me about the love I had for Boo Boo, I often tell them that it was the depth of love I held for her that was so surprising. My love for my children was expected — it's a natural, inherent part of being a parent. There's no surprise in loving your children so deeply.

But with a dog, it is entirely different and wholly unexpected. It's one of those things in life that you just don't understand until you experience it yourself.

Looking back, I can wholeheartedly say that loving Boo Boo was one of the greatest honors of my life. She became my best friend and a source of endless joy and comfort. The lessons she taught me about love and caring for another living being have stayed with me and shaped who I am today. So, while I may struggle to articulate perfectly the profound impact Boo Boo had on my life, I know that those who have shared their lives with a special dog will understand. They'll know that rare bond, that unique blend of love and friendship that makes saying goodbye hard but having them in our lives incredibly rewarding.

Reflecting on the journey I've been through; one truth stands out starkly in my mind: Boo Boo saved my life. It's as straightforward and as profound as that. Looking back with the clarity of hindsight, I can see the wisdom in what Denise did. It wasn't just a whimsical decision to bring a dog into our home; it was a well-thought-out plan, a strategy born out of her deep love and understanding of me. Denise knew that a dog would be good for me, far more than I ever realized at the time. She recognized that the responsibility of walking Boo Boo would not only get me out of the house but it would also serve as a much-needed distraction from my addiction to pills. It was about creating a new routine, a new focus in my life that was healthier and more positive. And beyond that, it was about giving me a new purpose, a reason to look forward to each day with something other than the struggles in my mind.

Her plan worked. The simple act of caring for Boo Boo, of ensuring her well-being, gradually shifted my focus away from my own troubles. It was therapeutic in a way I had never imagined possible.

I am forever grateful to Denise for her foresight and unwavering support. Her ability to love me, take care of me, and intuitively know what was best for me is just one of the myriad reasons why I love her so deeply. She saw a path to healing that I couldn't see for myself, and she gently guided me onto it.

The Road to Recovery

Boo Boo was the inspiration I needed to seek help from an addiction doctor. Now, you might naturally wonder, why wasn't my relationship with Denise, my kids, or my grandchildren the one that spurred this crucial decision? I've often pondered this question, turning it over in my mind and trying to understand the dynamics myself. Though seemingly straightforward, the answer carries a lot of weight in my heart. The truth is Denise, my children, and my grandchildren, as much as they mean to me, have always been strong, independent individuals. They each have their own lives, support systems, and unique ways of coping with the world. This strength of theirs, while a source of pride, also left me feeling somewhat peripheral in their lives. I never felt like they were dependent on me in the same way Boo Boo was.

This little puppy, with her complete reliance on me for her well-being, care, and companionship, created a different kind of responsibility — new and all-encompassing for me. For the first time in a long time, I felt unequivocally needed. Boo Boo's dependence on me was immediate and tangible; she needed me to feed her, walk her, and provide her with love and safety. This sense of being needed was a powerful motivator. It made me realize that to take care of Boo Boo in the way she deserved, I first needed to take care of myself.

Boo Boo wasn't just the spark that led me to seek out a real doctor to help with my addiction; she became my inspiration, my reason to fully commit to the recovery process. For the first time, I found myself not only willing, but eager to follow the doctor's instructions to the letter. These instructions, this guidance, were my lifeline — the path I needed to take to break free from the incredible, suffocating hold that opioids had on my life.

It's funny, isn't it? How can such a small creature have such a monumental impact? Boo Boo, with her innocent eyes and unconditional love, made me see the importance of not just surviving but thriving — for her sake as well as my own. I wanted to be there for her in every way possible, and that meant being healthy, being present, and being free from the chains of addiction.

The road to recovery was by no means easy. It was filled with challenges and setbacks, moments of doubt, and periods of struggle. But every time I looked at Boo Boo; every time I saw her wagging tail and felt her warmth, I was reminded of why I was on this journey. The instructions from the doctor — the treatment plans, the lifestyle changes, the therapy sessions — all became integral parts of my daily life.

The transformation I began to experience was remarkable. The changes, both physical and mental, started to manifest almost immediately. One of the first things I noticed was that I began to lose weight. It was as if the weight of my past struggles was being lifted off my shoulders. Each day, I felt healthier, more energetic, and genuinely happier.

But the changes weren't just limited to my personal health. In 2008, when the recession hit businesses hard, my own business was no exception. We faced challenges, uncertainties, and the same economic pressures impacting businesses everywhere. Yet, despite these difficulties, we managed to pull through with a revenue of a little more than 20 million dollars. It wasn't easy, but the newfound strength and clarity I gained from my recovery played a crucial role in navigating those tough times.

Feeling stronger, sharper, and more in tune with my capabilities, I could focus on my work like never before. I was working hard, but more importantly, I was working smarter.

This renewed vigor and strategic approach allowed us to significantly increase our revenue. In just a few years, as I progressed in my recovery and grew stronger in my resolve, our business flourished, reaching a remarkable milestone of 411 million dollars.

Looking back, I see these achievements not just as business successes but as tangible representations of the positive changes in my life. My journey of recovery, marked by better health and a clearer mind, was paralleled by the growth and success of my business. It was as if, as I rebuilt myself from the inside, everything around me started to align in a more positive and prosperous direction.

As I journeyed through my recovery and our lives began to change, one of the most heartwarming developments was how our blended family, my three daughters and Denise's two sons, started genuinely having fun together. We're blessed with 10 grandchildren whom we cherish and we began celebrating holidays together, which turned into something extraordinary. We started hosting sleepovers for the grandkids, which were always a hit. In the summer, everyone would come over to swim in our pool, and we loved having movie nights, too. Of course, Boo Boo was right in the middle of the action. She loved being around everyone, soaking up the attention and giving back as much love as she received. She was just one of the gang, always eager to join in on whatever was happening.

The Escape Artist

Boo Boo, with her adventurous spirit and boundless energy, certainly kept Denise and me on our toes. It's amusing now, looking back, how much she reminded us of the saying about cats having nine lives. Sometimes I wonder if Boo Boo was a cat in a past life, considering the number of escapades she had. We actually "lost" her about six times. She had a knack for wandering off, always finding some ingenious way to slip out of the house when we least expected it. Each time she disappeared, our hearts would sink, and we would spring into action.

We'd go around the neighborhood, hanging signs on every lamp post and tree we could find. Those days when she was gone were pure torture for us. But then, just when we started to lose hope, we'd receive a phone call – someone had found Boo Boo and had seen our sign.

Denise and I would rush over to the caller's house, sometimes finding that Boo Boo had traveled miles away from home. And there she would be, running up to us with what I can only describe as a mischievous, triumphant look on her face. It was as if she was playing an elaborate game of hide and seek, and in her mind, she was always the winner. She had this "cat who ate the canary" look, so proud of herself and her little adventure.

Despite the stress and worry of those times when she ran off, I gradually came to trust that Boo Boo would always find her way back to us. It was as if an invisible thread connected her to our family, guiding her home. Each time she returned; it reinforced my belief that she was meant to be with us.

Looking back at those escapades, they almost seem comical now, part of the rich tapestry of memories we've created with Boo Boo. She brought excitement and chaos, but most importantly, an abundance of love and laughter into our lives. Her wandering spirit was just another facet of her unique personality, a reminder of her embodied joy and spontaneity. As hard as it was during those times, I wouldn't change a thing. Boo Boo, in her own way, taught us about patience, trust, and the unbreakable bond we shared.

Nine Lives

Boo Boo had her fair share of mishaps too. One particular incident stands out in my memory, a time that shook me. We were driving, just me and her, and I had let her put her head out the window, something she absolutely loved to do. But on this occasion, something went wrong. She darted in the wrong way, and before I could even react, she fell out of the car window. Oh my God, the panic and fear coursing through me at that moment were overwhelming.

She was pretty severely hurt from the fall — a broken paw, several stitches, and a collection of bruises. Seeing her in that state, so vulnerable and in pain, just about broke my heart. She had to wear this apparatus to keep her from moving too much to ensure her injuries would heal properly. She absolutely hated it, of course. She would look at me with those sad eyes, and I could tell she was wondering why I had put her in this situation.

That incident weighed heavily on me because I knew it was my fault. I wasn't watching her as carefully as I should have been. The guilt I felt was immense. It was a stark reminder of my responsibility to keep her safe. From that day on, I never let her put her head out of the window again. The risk was just too great, and the memory of that accident was a constant, painful reminder. But through it all, she showed such resilience and spirit, even when she was laid up and healing.

At our lake house, we had some moments with Boo Boo that really tested our nerves. The area around the house was teeming with wildlife, especially deer. They would often come out to play in the back, and for Boo Boo, that was like an open invitation for a chase. No matter how much I tried to stop her, chasing those deer seemed her absolute favorite thing to do. She had this unbridled enthusiasm every time she saw them, her tail wagging furiously, eyes fixed on her playful targets.

One day, a situation unfolded that I'll never forget. It started like any other playful chase, with Boo Boo darting after the deer. But this time, something different happened. I remember watching in horror as one of the deer, perhaps feeling threatened or just annoyed by the chase, suddenly turned and started charging towards Boo Boo. My heart was in my throat as I saw this happening, powerless to intervene. The deer, much faster and stronger, quickly caught up with Boo Boo. In a moment that seemed to happen in slow motion but was over in an instant, the deer head-butted Boo Boo, sending her flying into the air. I can't begin to describe the fear and panic that gripped me. Watching her small body being thrown like that was one of the most terrifying experiences I've ever had.

I rushed over to her, my mind racing with worry about how badly she might be injured. Thankfully, Boo Boo was shaken but not seriously hurt. That incident, however, changed how we managed her outdoor activities. We became more cautious, constantly vigilant, to make sure she didn't put herself in harm's way again.

Boo Boo, clearly, was one tough little dog. Despite her small size, she had a stronger spirit than many I've known. Each time she encountered trouble or got hurt, it was astonishing how she would just shake it off and dive right back into her adventures. It's incredible how she managed to get away with all those shenanigans. Denise and I often joked that she must have had a guardian angel looking out for her. It felt like some kind of divine intervention was at play, not quite enough to keep her from finding trouble, but just enough to ensure she always came through whatever misadventure she had thrown herself into. This resilience of hers, this indomitable spirit, had allowed Boo Boo to live her life to the fullest without any fear or hesitation.

First Child/Only Child

Since Boo Boo joined us at the very beginning of our marriage, it was as if she was our child. And like any first addition to a family, she was spoiled. Boy, did we spoil her! Boo Boo had a particular fondness for those little dog toys you find in local stores like CVS or Walgreens. She had quite the collection, but her absolute favorites were the plush toys, especially the ones with buttons on their hands or feet that made them dance. She would grab one of those dancing toys, twist and turn it with her paws and mouth, making it dance. The concentration and joy on her face as she played were priceless.

Boo Boo's favorite activity, though, was to take walks with me. It was like magic how she responded to the word "walk." She could be in the deepest of sleeps, but the moment I mentioned a walk, her ears would perk up, and she'd be wide awake, tail wagging with anticipation. Our walking routine became a cherished part of both our days. We would walk every morning and twice on Saturdays and Sundays.

One of our favorite destinations was Seneca Park. I would drive there but had to park along a busy road. Despite the traffic and the distractions, Boo Boo never ran into the road. She seemed to understand the dangers and always stayed close by my side, patiently waiting as I locked the car and prepared for our walk.

Walking by the golf course at Seneca Park was a special treat, especially when it was quiet, and no golfers were around. We would sometimes stroll onto the grass, but if I saw someone and we needed to get off, she would immediately respond to my command. She knew my voice and my commands, and she respected them.

Boo Boo was a regular fixture at my office. Every workday, I'd look at her and say, "Boo Boo, let's go to work," and her reaction was always the same — a burst of energy, her tail wagging excitedly as she headed for the door.

The moment we arrived at the office, Boo Boo would transform into the unofficial greeter. With a joyous energy, she'd scamper around to everyone's office, a furry little ambassador making her rounds. She had this adorable way of saying "hi" to everyone, eagerly seeking out belly rubs, which she received in abundance. The smiles she brought to people's faces were indeed something special.

Once she had made sure everyone had a chance to greet her, Boo Boo would trot back to my office, where I always had a few treats waiting for her as a reward for her morning rounds. After enjoying her treats, she'd settle in the bed I had set up for her under my desk. It was her cozy spot where she'd relax and chill for the rest of the day.

Some days, she'd seem to think it was time to go home as early as 10 a.m., but she gradually learned that wasn't how the workday schedule went. Since Boo Boo would be relatively sedentary throughout the workday, I made it a point to wake up extra early to take her on a nice, long walk before heading to the office. I've never been a fan of waking up early, but for Boo Boo, it was worth it.

When it came to bedtime, Boo Boo had her own bed on the floor of our room, where she was supposed to sleep. Most nights, she had a different idea. She often jumped onto our bed and made herself comfortable near our feet. Somehow though, Denise usually woke up to find Boo Boo right above her head, on the top part of her pillow.

Bringing Boo Boo along with us wherever we went became second nature. She was such a vital part of our lives that it felt strange not to have her by our side. Whenever there was an occasion where we couldn't take her along, let me tell you, she made her feelings known upon our return. It was as if she was saying, "Talk to the paw," until we had sufficiently made it up to her.

Boo Boo was particularly fond of our lake house. It was one of her favorite places, and she absolutely loved coming on our boat with us. Given her adventurous spirit, I was always concerned about keeping her safe on the boat. But over time, she showed a remarkable ability to adapt and learn. Despite her natural inclination for wanderlust, Boo Boo developed a sense of responsibility and safety while on the boat.

There's something about a dog's unconditional love that touches the soul, especially after a hard day. For me, Boo Boo was the epitome of that love. No matter what kind of day I had, she was there, her presence a constant source of comfort and joy. She always wanted to do whatever I was doing and be right by my side. That feeling when I looked into her eyes, the one when I felt struck by a dart in my heart ... I felt that always. Every single time. It was, at times, overwhelming.

My relationship with Boo Boo truly transformed not just my personal life but also reshaped my perspective on the broader importance of caring for animals. This profound bond we shared opened my eyes to the needs of other animals and their owners who might not be as fortunate. That's why I've strongly supported animal charities, mainly focusing on helping with animal surgery centers.

I often think about the anguish and helplessness people must feel when their beloved pet needs surgery, a chance at survival, or a better quality of life, but the cost is just beyond their reach. Can you imagine the depth of despair that would cause? Knowing that your dog or cat, a family member, could be saved with a procedure, but the financial burden is too much to bear? It's a heartbreaking scenario, one that too many people face. So, I donate to these animal surgery centers, aiming to assist those who find themselves in such dire situations. It's a way for me to give back, to extend the same kind of love and care that Boo Boo gave me to other animals and their families. No one should have to make the impossible choice between financial stability and their pet's health.

Supporting these charities has become a passion of mine, a way to keep the spirit of what Boo Boo taught me alive. She showed me the depth of the bond between a person and their pet, and now, I want to help preserve and protect that bond for others. It's a commitment that brings a sense of fulfillment and purpose, knowing that in some small way, I'm contributing to the well-being of animals and providing relief to their owners in their time of need.

Boo Boo had this uncanny ability to sense the mood in our home, especially between Denise and me. It was quite remarkable, really. Whenever Denise and I had a disagreement, Boo Boo could tell, and she didn't like it one bit. You could see it in her behavior — she'd become quieter, almost as if trying to soothe the atmosphere with her calming presence.

Equally impressive was her ability to sense when I wasn't feeling well. On days when I was under the weather, needing to rest and recuperate, Boo Boo would be right there by my side. She transformed into the most low-maintenance companion you could imagine. Instead of her usual playful self, she would simply rest with me, offering her quiet support. It was as if she understood that what I needed most was her presence, her silent companionship.

When Boo Boo needed medical attention, however, things were a little different. I remember once she had an ear infection, and I had to put medicine in her ear. If I said to Denise, "Hey, can you bring over Boo Boo's medicine," Boo Boo would instantly know what was coming. She would take off like a shot, hiding under the bed and wriggling right to the middle where we couldn't reach her. It was as if she understood every word we were saying. The intelligence and understanding she displayed always amazed me.

This experience with Boo Boo reinforced my belief that companion animals are highly intelligent beings. They possess a deep understanding and an emotional intelligence that often goes unrecognized. Boo Boo, like many animals, seemed to have an awareness, an innate sense of the world around her that was truly remarkable. I often thought that animals, in their own way, have a path just like us — a journey to grow, learn, and ascend.

The realization that Boo Boo relied on me to be healthy and well so that I could take proper care of her ensured my steadfast compliance with my doctor's orders. Of course, the path to recovery was not without its challenges. Every once in a while, I would experience a minor setback, a momentary hurdle that curtailed my progress a little bit. But, inspired by Boo Boo's unwavering loyalty and love, I never allowed these setbacks to deter me. Instead, they served as reminders of my journey and the importance of staying the course. No matter how small, each step was a step in the right direction.

Recovery

I am filled with a deep sense of pride and accomplishment when I look back and remember reaching the milestone of full recovery in April 2008. My life, once derailed by opioid addiction, had come full circle back on track, and it felt absolutely fantastic. Denise, Boo Boo, and I were living this beautiful, fulfilling life together, a life that was once a distant dream during my darker days. It's remarkable how things turned around, how the pieces of my life fell into place.

I continued on my path to better health, steadily losing weight, a physical manifestation of the positive changes I made. It wasn't just about the numbers on the scale; it was about feeling healthier, more energetic, and more alive than I had in years. This transformation reminded me of where I had been and how far I had come.

Meanwhile, my business, which had weathered the storm of my personal struggles, flourished. We were making millions, a testament to the hard work, dedication, and renewed focus I could bring to it post-recovery. The business's success was not just a personal achievement but a source of stability and security for my family, which gave me a great sense of self-satisfaction.

One of the most gratifying aspects of having my life back on track was the quality time I could spend with my three beautiful daughters, their husbands, and my grandchildren. Being present in their lives, watching the grandkids grow, and being part of their milestones and everyday moments was incredibly rewarding.

Additionally, I found the time to indulge in my passions and hobbies. Perhaps most significantly, I returned to my joy of reading. During my addiction, this had fallen by the wayside. I was now able to immerse myself in a multitude of worlds through my books.

A New Path

In May 2015, I experienced a loss that deeply affected me. Randy Jackson, a close friend of my family, died. Randy was like an uncle to me, close to my dad. Randy's son actually worked for me. Randy was the United States Director of Kia Motor Manufacturing in Georgia, and his death was sudden and unexpected. I found myself grappling with a range of emotions, from disbelief to profound sadness. His presence had been a significant part of my life, and his sudden departure left me searching for answers, for some sense of closure. In my quest for understanding, I did something I had never done before: I visited a psychic. I was driven by a need to know more about his death than what was published in the papers or the information that was relayed to me. I was hoping to find some peace, some understanding that could help me process this loss.

As soon as the psychic walked into the room, the experience took an unexpected turn. Without any preamble, she declared that I was a healer. This took me by surprise; it was not what I had come in to hear, but her words struck a chord within me.

She then asked if I would like to meet one of my spirit guides. I was intrigued, and I agreed despite not knowing entirely what to expect.

Saying yes was a leap into the unknown, a realm I had never explored. It marked the beginning of a new chapter in my journey, one that would open my eyes to different perspectives and possibilities. It was a testament to how life can take unexpected turns, guiding us toward new experiences and insights, even amid grief.

Embarking on this path of exploration opened up a whole new world for me, both intriguing and deeply personal. The experience with the psychic, the notion of being a healer, and the idea of spirit guides all sparked a curiosity I had never quite felt before. I wanted to delve deeper, understand how to communicate with the other side, and get in touch with my higher self. It was a journey calling out to me, inviting me to explore realms beyond the tangible.

As a result, my reading choices began to shift significantly. I found myself drawn to books and writings on spiritual topics, seeking knowledge and insight into areas I had never considered. This newfound interest was not just about gathering information; it was a quest for understanding, a search for meaning in the grand scheme of things.

For the first time in my life, I grappled with questions that touched on the essence of existence. Questions like, "Why am I here? What is my purpose in this life?" seemed to resonate deep within my soul. I pondered what I could leave behind for my grandchildren, the kind of legacy that would be meaningful and enduring.

The mysteries of life and death also occupied my thoughts. "What happens when we die? What lies on the other side?" These questions, once distant thoughts, now felt urgently relevant. I wondered about the existence of angels and whether I had any watching over me. The possibility of such guardians gave me comfort, yet I yearned to know more, to understand their presence in our lives.

The most pressing question, however, was about communication with these spiritual entities. "How do I communicate with them, and more importantly, how do I know they are communicating with me?" This became a central focus of my spiritual journey. It wasn't just about belief or faith; it was about seeking a tangible connection, a way to interact and understand the messages that I felt were beyond my grasp.

This exploration period was not just an intellectual exercise but a deeply emotional and spiritual journey. It was about connecting with something greater than myself and understanding the unseen forces that guide and shape our lives. It opened up a new realm of possibilities. It provided a sense of connectedness to the universe I had never experienced. This path of exploration, prompted by the loss of a dear friend and the unexpected guidance of a psychic, led me to question, seek, and discover aspects of life and existence that brought new depth and meaning to my everyday experiences.

It's a bit strange, really, how life works sometimes. There I was, finally, at a point in my life where I wasn't plagued by worries about dying. Because of my support system and my relationship with Boo Boo, I had come such a long way — I was healthy again, not just physically, but also in mind and spirit. I had conquered my addiction, reconnected with my family, and my business was thriving. Everything seemed to fall into place, a harmonious balance I had longed for and worked hard to achieve. So, it did strike me as odd that amidst all this newfound stability and health, I found myself deeply curious about the afterlife.

This curiosity wasn't born out of fear or anxiety; instead, it felt like a natural, almost inevitable progression of my journey. I pondered why, at this juncture of my life, I was suddenly drawn to these profound existential questions. It was as if a new door had opened, revealing a path I was meant to explore.

As I delved deeper into these spiritual inquiries, the pieces came together. I realized that this curiosity and exploration led me to discover my true purpose. It wasn't just about satisfying a newfound interest; it was about embarking on a journey that would fundamentally change the trajectory of my life.

Denise, myself, and our Boo Boo

Chapter 3

Healing Mary, Healing Tim

Isn't it astonishing that all these secrets have been preserved for so many years just so we could discover them.

Orville Wright

Embarking on this new spiritual journey was a transformative experience for me. It was like becoming a whole new version of myself, Tim 2.0, and the sense of upliftment was profound. I felt not just good but on a path to complete healing. With each question I explored, I delved deeper into learning, and the excitement was palpable. I was genuinely happy, embracing this newfound spiritual exploration with open arms. However, it wasn't long before I noticed that not everyone in my life was as enthusiastic about this journey as I was, particularly Denise.

My partner Denise was closest to me, yet it became increasingly apparent that she did not share my excitement. My daughters, too, were initially skeptical, labeling my interests and pursuits as odd. But Denise's hesitance hit closer to home, creating a tangible rift in our relationship. We found ourselves diverging in our interests and preferences, from how we spent our free time to what we found engaging to read, watch, or discuss.

At the heart of my new path was a deep dive into meditation, spirituality, angels, spirit guides, and afterlife concepts. I voraciously read up on these subjects, connected with individuals who shared similar beliefs, and sought guidance from spiritual leaders and mentors. This spiritual awakening was crucial to me and was the first step in becoming a "lightworker."

What Is a Lightworker?

The concept of lightworkers emerged in the spiritual community as individuals who are deeply drawn to helping others and the planet. Originating from the teachings of Michael Mirdad in the early 1980s and further popularized by Doreen Virtue in 1997 through her book *The Lightworker's Way,* lightworkers are seen as spiritual beings committed to serving humanity. They are often described by using terms such as crystal babies, indigos, Earth angels, and star seeds, each embodying the mission to spread light and love.

Lightworkers are characterized by their innate compassion and empathy, often displaying a strong desire to aid others from a young age. This might manifest in simple acts like rescuing animals or more complex human interactions. Their sensitivity makes them acutely aware of the world's suffering. It drives them towards professions where they can make a difference, such as healthcare, therapy, education, and other caregiving roles.

These individuals rely on their intuition and internal guidance to navigate their path, using their abilities to sense and alleviate the emotional and physical pain of others. Lightworkers believe in collective efforts to combat negative energies and promote healing through positive action. If you resonate with these characteristics, feel a profound connection to all beings, and desire to assist those in need, you might be exploring the path of a lightworker. This journey involves tapping into your unique abilities and determining how best you can serve, whether through direct healing, psychic insights, communication, or other means of spreading light and positivity.

Lightworkers can specialize in various areas, from healing and guidance to more esoteric roles like manifesting. Some focus on communicating essential messages or ideas to inspire and uplift humanity, while others work more energetically to cleanse negativity and support the collective consciousness' evolution.

Ultimately, being a lightworker is about recognizing your potential to make a difference and finding ways to manifest this purpose in your life, regardless of its specific form. It's a call to live authentically, align with your highest values, and contribute to the world's healing and transformation. It is a beacon of hope and love in whatever resonates with your soul.

Divergent Paths

As strong as my desire was to continue on this path, Denise remained apprehensive. Her concerns were rooted in fear, particularly the fear of the unknown and the potentially negative perceptions of others. She worried about the implications of my spiritual practices, even going so far as to express fear that my activities could invite unwelcome or malevolent forces into our home. Her lack of understanding clearly represented a significant obstacle in our relationship.

This disconnect was more than just a minor disagreement; it indicated a fundamental divergence in our paths. What I was coming to see as essential and transformative in my life held little to no interest for Denise. This growing gap between us was challenging, to say the least. Despite my deep love for her, it was hard to ignore that we were moving in opposite directions, driven by vastly different interests and values. For her, the journey that brought me so much fulfillment and joy was a source of concern and misunderstanding.

On a particular Saturday in autumn 2017, I found myself with a strong desire to meditate, more potent than usual. It would have been great if I could have set up a dedicated space in our home, but it wasn't the right place. My phone was ringing all the time, Boo Boo was always running around; it just wasn't a conducive environment. Instead, I often sought guidance from my spirit guides on where to find peace and quiet for meditation. That day, they were directing me towards the park.

Upon arriving at the park, I was immediately disappointed by the noise of lawnmowers cutting the grass, disrupting the peace I sought. Determined, I left and drove to St. Agnes, my local church, hoping for a quieter environment. However, as soon as I stepped out of my car, I was greeted by the sound of another lawn mower. Frustrated, I muttered to myself and walked to the opposite end of the parking lot. I noticed many people walking towards something, so I followed them, only to find a sign for the "Earth & Spirit Center" — a discovery that felt almost too serendipitous. Intrigued, I looked it up online and was excited to learn that they offered meditation, mindfulness, and social justice programs, among many others.

Feeling inspired, I began exploring the area, looking for spots where I could finally meditate. Even though I found myself walking to my church, I impulsively chose a slightly different path I had never walked before. This path led me to a circle of bushes about seven feet tall. It was odd because these bushes were in an area where Brother Jerry cut the grass every week. It was about 30 yards from the back of the church and 10 yards from the road. It struck me as odd that these bushes were never paid attention to. They were overgrown and seemed more out of place than the manicured lawn. Curious, I walked to them to take a closer look, and I couldn't believe my eyes — I found a statue hidden behind the greenery. To my astonishment, it was a statue of the Blessed Mother in all her glory.

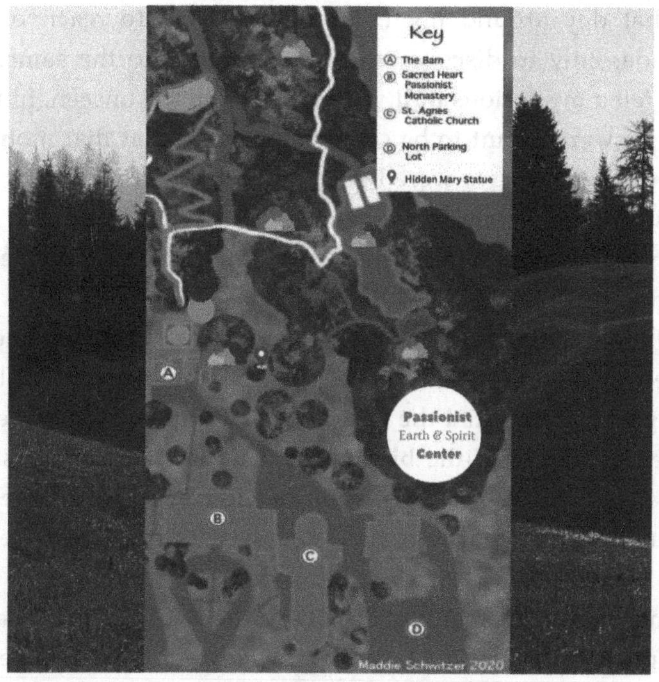

I couldn't help but wonder about its history — how long had it been there, why was it left obscured by bushes, and why was I the one to find it? Interpreting this discovery as a clear sign, I felt more assured than ever about continuing my spiritual journey. In a gesture of respect and to share this find with others, I hired a yard service to clear the bushes around her, allowing sunlight to illuminate her beauty and making her visible for others to appreciate.

Two weeks later, on an ordinary morning that would soon prove anything but, I felt a peculiar calling, a whisper of something more waiting to be identified. At this time, I was part of a spiritual group. This community sought deeper meanings and connections beyond the physical realm. Rhonda Etherton, introduced to me by my daughter Tori, led the group and was my first spiritual mentor.

That day around noon, I felt compelled to reach out to Rhonda, only to discover she was about to do the same. We both felt a mysterious pull, a directive from the unseen, hinting that we were meant to be somewhere specific at that moment. Rhonda believed we were being called to St. Agnes. That was unusual because she only knew of St. Agnes because I had recently told her about my discovery of the statue of the Blessed Mother.

Upon our arrival, we were greeted by the sight of the newly unveiled statue – the bushes cleared that very day. Even though I had initiated the clearing, I had not been informed of the exact timing of the big reveal. The Blessed Mother stood tall, an embodiment of perseverance and a beacon of numerous spiritual virtues that resonated deeply with those who beheld her.

In the initial moments of discovery, the awe that enveloped us was pure and untainted by any knowledge of the date's deeper meaning. Yet, as we stood there, captivated by the statue's serene presence, it seemed the universe was orchestrating an intricate dance of synchronicities. Unbeknownst to us, unveiling the statue on this specific day was a nod to a grander cosmic plan.

The day, October 13th, held layers of historical and mystical importance that we were yet to uncover. In its infinite wisdom, the universe had chosen this moment to bridge the past with the present, inviting us into a space where time folded upon itself, revealing connections that transcended our immediate understanding.

As Rhonda and I absorbed the quiet majesty of the statue, we could not help but feel that the universe had conspired to bring us here, to this exact spot, at this precise moment. The significance of the date, the unexpected unveiling of the statue, and the presence of the Blessed Mother herself were all pieces of a puzzle that we were just beginning to assemble, which promised to unlock new realms of understanding and insight.

What was the significance of October 13th? It marked the 100th anniversary of the Blessed Mother's final apparition at Fatima to three children in Portugal in 1917.

And the Story Goes

According to the Lady of Fatima Catholic Church, the story begins in Fatima, Portugal, on May 13th, 1917. *On that fateful day near that tiny village, the Blessed Virgin Mary, Mother of God, appeared to three young peasant children: Francisco, Jacinta, and Lucia, ages 10, 9, and 7. As was the custom, these youngsters were tending their family's sheep when "a Lady all in white, more brilliant than the sun ... indescribably beautiful," standing above a bush, appeared to them.*

From May through October 1917, the Lady appeared and spoke to the children on the 13th day of each month. News of these apparitions began to spread throughout the region. The children recounted that the Virgin told them that God had sent her with a message for every man, woman, and child living in the century. She promised that God would grant the world peace if Her requests for prayer, reparation, and consecration were heard and obeyed. While many believed the children had seen the Virgin, others discounted their story, subjecting them to much derision and ridicule. When it became known the Lady would visit the children for the last time on October 13th, 1917, and had promised a sign that would convince the world she had appeared, many pilgrims made plans to attend.

Though the region had been subjected to three days of torrential downpours, nearly 70,000 people journeyed through the heavy rain and mud to the place of the previous apparitions to witness the predicted miracle. Many were scornful unbelievers whose sole intent was to discredit the children's stories.

Suddenly, the "clouds separated ... and the sun appeared between them in the clear blue, like a disk of white fire." The people could look at the sun without blinking, and while they gazed upward, the giant ball began to "dance." The considerable fireball whirled rapidly with dizzy and sickening speed, flinging out all sorts of brilliant colors that reflected on the faces of the crowds. The fiery ball continued to gyrate thrice, then seemed to tremble and shudder and plunge in a mighty zigzag course toward the earth. The crowd was terrified, fearing this was the end of the world.

However, the sun reversed course and, retracing its zigzagging course, returned to its usual place in the heavens. All of this transpired in approximately 10 minutes. After realizing they were not doomed, the crowd began laughing, crying, shouting, and weeping. Many discovered their previously drenched clothing to be perfectly dry.

After what was known as "The Miracle of the Sun," the children were grilled many times about what they had seen and been told. Their story never changed. The heart of Our Lady's message to the world is contained in what has become known as the "Secret," which she confided to the children in July 1917. The "Secret" actually consists of three parts. The first part of the "Secret" was a frightening vision of hell, "where the souls of poor sinners go," and contained an urgent plea from Our Lady for acts of prayer and sacrifice to save souls, with particular emphasis on praying of the rosary and devotion to the Immaculate Heart of Mary.

The second part of the "Secret" specifically prophesied the outbreak of World War II and contained the prediction of the immense damage that Russia would do to humanity by abandoning the Christian faith and embracing Communist totalitarianism.

The third part was not revealed until 2000. Its revelation coincided with the beatification of Francisco and Jacinta. It did not contain any striking or cataclysmic prediction. Still, instead, the vision supported and affirmed the immense suffering endured by witnesses of the faith in the last century of the second millennium. Sister Lucia, the surviving member of the Fatima trio, confirmed that in the vision, "the Bishop clothed in white," who prays for all the faithful, is the Pope. As he makes his way with great difficulty towards the Cross amid the corpses of those who were martyred (bishops, priests, men and women religious, and many lay people), he too falls to the ground, apparently dead, under a hail of gunfire. It is possible that the vision predicted the 1981 attack on Pope John Paul II's life. The Pope has always credited the Virgin for his survival.

The Blessed Mary enshrouded, discovered, and uncovered. I am honored to pose with her.

The statue of the Blessed Mother is reputed to possess healing energies, so I affectionately call her "Healing Mary." She inspired me to engage in meditation sessions focused on tapping into these energies. However, meditating outdoors is only feasible under specific weather conditions, leading me to also seek guidance indoors. My search for deeper spiritual engagement was aided by Rhonda. Rhonda has a wealth of experience working with various energies, making her an ideal guide for my spiritual journey.

Working with Rhonda marked a turning point in my exploration of spirituality. She was instrumental in elevating my understanding and practice to a new level. One of her first recommendations was to read the book entitled *Ramtha: The White Book,* which she believed would significantly benefit me. Taking her advice, I found that the book was indeed transformative. *Ramtha* offers profound insights into the essence of our being and existence in a unique and enlightening way.

The teachings of *Ramtha* have had a lasting impact on my life, giving me a perspective on my identity and purpose that was previously unexplored. This book and Rhonda's mentorship have been pivotal in shaping my spiritual path. They have challenged me to look deeper into my existence's nature and understand myself in ways I had not considered before.

Denise and I were still at odds over my life's new direction. During this tumultuous phase in my marriage, I found myself engulfed in solitude and despair. "Is there somebody who can help me?" I would cry to myself. My interest in spiritual guidance had already set me on the path to connecting with my spirit guides. Still, nothing could have prepared me for what happened next. Around 3:00 a.m., a time reputed for spiritual visions, I experienced something extraordinary – an out-of-body journey led by my spirit guides.

Twin Flames

This nocturnal voyage took me back to a past life in India. Dressed in a uniform, I was driving a truck along a picturesque landscape towards a striking body of water. My destination was a solitary building adjacent to this serene setting. Upon arrival, I entered the building where I encountered Carol, a spirit guide who I quickly discovered was my guide of joy and pleasure. She is my twin flame, the eternal connector bound to me across lifetimes. Before delving deeper into our connection, exploring the concept of twin flames is crucial.

The twin flame journey, as explored by Emily Jennings in her book *Twin Flame Transcendence: The Spiritual Journey of Twin Flames,* delves into the transformative power of adversity in personal and spiritual growth. She presents the path of twin flames as one marked by significant challenges, including heartache and suffering. These difficulties are not mere obstacles but pivotal experiences that catalyze deep inner development and a greater understanding of oneself and the universe.

Jennings invites readers to reconsider their existing beliefs about twin flames. She expands the concept beyond the conventional romantic narrative, suggesting that twin flames embody a profound spiritual connection. This redefinition encourages individuals to view their twin flame experiences through a broader, more spiritual lens, opening the door to a richer, more nuanced understanding of these connections.

She emphasizes the nonlinear nature of the twin flame journey, recognizing that each individual's path is distinct. This journey does not adhere to a set sequence or timeline. Still, it unfolds in a way that is unique to each person, reflecting their own spiritual needs and lessons.

In her exploration, Jennings breaks down the twin flame experience into segments of identification, understanding, and finding spiritual purpose. This structured approach aids individuals in navigating the complexities of their twin flame relationships, providing a roadmap for exploring and interpreting the profound connections and challenges they encounter.

Much of Jennings' work is devoted to the importance of self-love and inner work. She argues that the twin flame journey is as much about personal awakening and growth as it is about connecting with one another. Through meditation and other spiritual practices, individuals are encouraged to delve into self-exploration and healing, managing the intense energies often accompanying twin flame connections.

Jennings also redefines twin flame relationships to encompass more than just a physical or romantic union. She highlights the importance of spiritual and energetic connections, suggesting that the true essence of a twin flame relationship lies in its ability to foster spiritual work and personal development.

Ultimately, Jennings presents the twin flame journey as integral to one's spiritual path. She posits that belief in and accepting this journey, with all its trials and tribulations, is essential. This perspective encourages individuals to embrace their twin flame experiences as opportunities for growth, learning, and spiritual evolution, reinforcing that the journey is as significant as its outcome.

Tanya Carroll Richardson adds to the discourse with her insights, suggesting that twin flames serve as mirrors, illuminating the parts of ourselves we often wish to avoid. However, she also cautions against narrowly viewing the twin flame concept, arguing that romantic fulfillment can come from multiple sources, not just a single destined partner. This perspective challenges the notion of perfection in relationships, advocating for a more balanced and realistic approach to love and personal fulfillment.

The twin flame journey is not just about finding romantic fulfillment but about personal growth, healing, and the realization that completeness comes from within.

In my vision, Carol approached me, her beauty striking. In that moment, and in all moments, she radiated a loveliness that's hard to put into words. When she embraced me, the emotional impact was so profound that it still tears my eyes to recall it. We found ourselves lying down on a couch in the room, and I remember crying for what felt like days. It's important to clarify that this experience had nothing to do with physical desire. My love and commitment to my wife are unwavering. However, when Denise and I were experiencing a deep disconnect, Carol's embrace provided the kind of support and nurturing I desperately needed.

The act of a spirit guide reaching out in such a genuine, supportive way might seem illogical to some. Yet, the comfort and connection I felt in that moment were beyond words, a sensation of profound beauty and relief. This moment with Carol wasn't about finding love or affection elsewhere. Still, it was about receiving the kind of human connection and understanding I was missing. It was a pure, deeply-needed sense of support during a challenging period.

This experience with Carol opened my eyes to the potential for healing and transformation through spiritual and emotional connections with others. The encounter was a turning point, leading me to explore other spiritually transformative events (STEs) that could offer similar profound insights and emotional healing. It underscored the power of human connection and the unexpected ways to find support and understanding from those around us.

Marriage Counseling

It was clear to Denise and me that this spiritual quest I was on would not end any time soon. We decided to seek help from a marriage counselor who came highly recommended, with three published books on relationships and marriage counseling to his name. His expertise was undeniable. He approached our sessions with a keen focus on understanding and resolving our issues. He guided us back towards a healthier path, aiming for a stronger and more successful relationship.

One particular piece of advice he gave us has had a lasting impact. Whenever we do something the other dislikes or fails to do something the other expected, we've learned to ask ourselves, "Was this an agreed-upon behavior, or was it just my expectation?" This simple question has proved incredibly effective at clarifying misunderstandings and addressing grievances without assigning blame or fostering resentment.

After our counseling sessions, Denise began understanding and accepting my spiritual pursuits. I continued attending my meditation group and consultations with spiritual advisors but with a newfound openness. I no longer felt the need to conceal my activities or interests. The judgment and skepticism that once shadowed my actions had dissipated. From the beginning of my spiritual journey to now, I have immersed myself in approximately 400–500 books, each contributing to my growth and understanding without the fear of criticism. This shift in our relationship dynamic, facilitated by our counselor's guidance, allowed me to fully embrace my path without compromising my home life.

The discovery of the Healing Mary statue profoundly transformed me. It opened my eyes and heart to messages and signs I previously might have ignored or not understood. I began to question and interpret the world around me differently: Could a flickering light be more than just an electrical issue? Was misplacing my keys a simple oversight or something more? And I felt those intuitive nudges – were they my thoughts or messages from spirit guides and angels, encouraging me to pay closer attention? This period in my life was marked by a growing sense of discernment, an awareness that the thoughts and feelings I experienced might not always be solely my own but could include communications meant to guide me.

Healing Mary's Message

Upon finding the Healing Mary, I felt an unmistakable message: she was inviting me to care for her, to bring her rosaries, and to use these rosaries as instruments of healing for others. It was a compelling feeling, an inner conviction that she wanted me to extend healing love to those in desperate need. To honor this calling, I continue to bring rosaries and flowers to her statue, where I pray and meditate. This devotion has become a cornerstone of my faith and belief in the divine, a clear sign that there's something greater at work beyond my own existence – a larger purpose and reason for everything.

This spiritually transformative experience with the Healing Mary was a pivotal moment, a realization of the vastness and depth of the divine. It prompted me to delve deeper into the history and significance of Marian apparitions, leading me to acquire books and learn more about the healing aspects often associated with these phenomena. Marian apparitions refer to the phenomena where the Blessed Virgin Mary is believed to descend from heaven to earth. These events typically involve Mary conveying a specific message, and the duration of her appearances can range from a single brief visit to multiple occurrences spanning years. Each apparition is witnessed by at least one individual, who often may be later venerated as a saint or revered figure within the Church. This exploration reinforced my belief in the importance of the rosaries I placed and the specific individuals I felt compelled to give them to.

My journey since discovering the Healing Mary has been one of constant learning and spiritual growth. I am driven by a desire to understand the reasons behind my connection to her and the broader implications of her appearances around the world. This path has deepened my faith and instilled in me a profound sense of purpose and commitment to spreading healing and love.

Around a year after discovering the statue of the Healing Mary, a close friend of mine was diagnosed with cancer. He battled the disease bravely for two years before his condition began to deteriorate. Around this time, I decided he would be the first person to whom I would give one of the rosaries, inspired by the message I felt from the Healing Mary. After visiting him at his home and giving him the rosary, I noticed something unusual as I was leaving. It was a rainy day, and as I looked into my car's rearview camera, I spotted an orb. I even captured a photo of it because it was so unexpected. I had never seen anything like that before, and I couldn't help but feel it held some significance, perhaps a sign of approval from the divine for giving the rosary to my friend.

My friend managed to hold on for another year after receiving the rosary, and he told me that he always kept it with him. Eventually, though, he passed away from cancer. Of course, it would have been a miraculous story if the rosary had somehow cured his cancer. Dealing with death and the deep sense of loss that comes with it is incredibly challenging.

Yet, as another of my mentors, Dr. Rebecca Martin, often discusses, there's a belief in a broader plan at work. It requires faith to see that there's a path for everyone and that death is not just an end but a transition. When people pass away, they shed their physical form, and their essence or light body remains. While it's painful to lose someone close, there's also a perspective that their passing could be seen as a transition to a peaceful and beautiful place.

Motivated by this belief and the initial experience with my friend, I've continued to give out rosaries on special occasions or to people who need them. Each time, it's an act of faith and a gesture that I hope brings comfort or peace to the person receiving it, even if it's in the face of something as challenging as a severe illness or the prospect of death.

I firmly believe in the interconnectedness of all beings. Every person in the universe is linked in some way. This connection extends to people entering and exiting our lives; there's always a reason behind these encounters. It could be tied to experiences from past lives, potential interactions in future lives, or hold some significance in our current existence. Understanding the nature of these connections can offer profound insights into our journey through life.

Finding the Healing Mary statue was no coincidence in my eyes. I'm convinced there's a deeper reason I stumbled upon her, a connection not only to the statue itself but also to the individuals responsible for placing it there. This belief is reinforced because it remained undiscovered and overlooked for many years despite its proximity to the Earth and Spirit Center, where classes and activities are regularly held. And remember, as a young boy, I swam and played quite near where it was hidden. Nobody, not even me, noticed her until I did as an adult. I find all of it quite extraordinary.

This discovery wasn't just a matter of being in the right place at the right time; it speaks to a specific connection and purpose that aligns with my spiritual journey. The unnoticed presence of the Healing Mary near a place dedicated to spiritual learning and growth, yet remaining hidden from others, underscores the uniqueness of my connection to it. I was destined to find it but only when I was ready to appreciate it. It suggests that there are paths we are meant to follow and discoveries we are destined to make, guided by connections that transcend our understanding.

Chapter 4
Lifting the Veil

There is no death, just a change of worlds.
Chief Seattle, 19th century leader

This is now a good juncture to discuss, in greater detail, my entry into the universe of orbs, lifting the veil on another world. Seeing the orb in my rearview mirror after leaving my friend's house was the first time I had such an experience. However, my deep dive into this exploration began with the striking moment I had when photographing Boo Boo on her deathbed, and seeing a green orb floating above her head. This event sparked an intense curiosity, leading me to investigate orbs more intently.

This chapter is also about more than my personal quest. It's about the human drive to explore and understand the unknown. It challenges me and hopefully you to consider our perceptions and beliefs about the unseen aspects of our world, perhaps lifting the veil into another world altogether.

Twinkling Bells

Rhonda introduced me to a woman named Cheryl Gentry. Just like Rhonda, Cheryl has played a significant role in my healing and spiritual growth. Funny enough, our initial connection came through massage therapy, which evolved into a deeper relationship.

Cheryl was intuitive and lived in a condo she thought was haunted by a ghost with a history of addiction. She used her home as a healing space for herself and her massage therapy clients. I found my visits to Cheryl very beneficial. She was adept at adjusting my body and posture. Our sessions included physical adjustments and discussions about spirituality. Cheryl offered valuable insights and advice on my spiritual journey.

One unusual experience we shared was hearing what seemed like twinkling bells during our sessions, a phenomenon we couldn't explain. This wasn't just any music – the best way to describe it is that it sounded like confetti falling from heaven. Whenever this occurred, Cheryl and I would acknowledge it, sometimes silently with a smile or simple nod. It was as if these moments were reminders of a past connection or the powerful synergy of our combined energies.

This phenomenon of the twinkling bells became a recurring event and bonded us until Cheryl's move to Arizona. Her departure was a poignant chapter's end to a story that had been filled with spiritual awakening and healing. However, the memory of those twinkling bells remains with me and will forever. It was my first venture into the realm of the mystical.

Saying Goodbye to My Best Friend

In 2020, Boo Boo started showing signs of decline. Her appetite diminished, and her strength waned. Our cherished routine, a Saturday morning walk at Seneca Golf Course, became difficult for her. Despite varying weather conditions, we never missed these walks for 15 years. Still, she eventually could no longer participate and sat quietly during our attempts.

As her condition worsened, we consulted our veterinarian, Dr. Shelley, who made a home visit to assess Boo Boo's health. Although it wasn't quite time to say goodbye during her first visit, Boo Boo's joy in life noticeably faded by early July of that year. Animals seem to have an innate understanding of when their time has come, preferring to avoid suffering and longing to reunite with their loved ones. They communicate a heartfelt message: they will cherish and miss us, but they are prepared to depart, urging us not to cling to them in pain. Acknowledging her suffering, we made the difficult decision to let her go peacefully. We didn't want her to suffer, not even for a second.

On a Friday afternoon, in the comfort of her favorite spot on our bed, Dr. Shelley helped us provide Boo Boo with a gentle passing. I had asked Dr. Shelley if it saddened her to do this agonizing work. She shared that it wasn't agonizing; she viewed her role as an honor, helping pets transition peacefully at home. This conversation highlighted the necessity of the act of letting go. Even though I couldn't fully appreciate it then, I can and do now.

Denise and I were there with her, feeling relief that her pain was ending but intense anguish at the same time. When it was over, I took a picture of Boo Boo and sobbed. Overwhelmed with grief, I sought refuge in my car, a place where I usually found comfort through music. However, this time, I was consumed by sorrow, driving aimlessly around while shouting to nobody, "NO!" I kept pounding on the steering wheel as if I thought that could somehow release the sense of loss.

The pain was so intense that I now actually avoid listening to the music that was playing at the time, as it brings back the torture of that moment. I was simply unable to accept that Boo Boo was no longer with me, and my reaction was a genuinely raw expression of my profound loss.

The year she passed away was undeniably the most challenging period of my life. Before she died, as everyone knows, the terrible year started with the outbreak of COVID-19. Boo Boo died in July. I struggled with denial and depression, and the bad streak of luck culminated when I was diagnosed with shingles at the end of August.

Shingles is excruciating. The pain is indescribable; it felt as though someone was extinguishing a cigarette on my skin. I couldn't bear anything touching the affected area. Although I would never seriously consider ending my life, if there were ever a moment that pushed me close to that edge, it was when I was suffering from shingles.

Light at the End of the Tunnel

The shingles lingered until the end of October. The physical trauma on the heels of losing my best friend took its toll on me. Luckily, finally, a glimmer of hope emerged the day I revisited the last picture I had taken of Boo Boo and noticed that green orb hovering above her.

I interpreted this as a sign, urging me to embark on a new path and to understand its significance. I've since learned that the color green symbolizes the human spirit or a connection with nature. Considering Boo Boo's deep affection for the outdoors, this connection felt particularly fitting. Boo Boo's presence has also manifested in orbs of various colors, not just green, suggesting a diversity of energies or aspects of her spirit.

Boo Boo was once again influencing and affecting my life, even though she was no longer physically by my side. I was inspired to delve deeper into the phenomena of orbs, quickly realizing they are not random occurrences but manifestations of spirit entities.

I began taking pictures in my backyard with simple tools like an iPhone camera. I soon realized that what looked like an orb was quite possibly just refractory light. So, I invested in more advanced technology and bought a Canon T6 high-definition camera and then a 4G video recorder, all in my quest to capture clearer images of orbs. My goal was not just to collect these images but to begin to understand what they might represent or communicate.

I began viewing orbs as potential carriers of messages or symbols from another world. I started capturing various orbs with unique color, movement, and presence. I questioned what these differences meant, considering how much of my observations are subjective and how much might be objective communication from the orbs themselves.

Sometimes, if the connection is strong, I can discern faces within these orbs, whether white, pink, green, blue, or even a mix of colors. In some videos, the background is almost entirely black, enhancing the visibility of the orbs and the souls they signify, moving and interacting in this captured otherworldly space.

Through my experiences with orbs in my backyard, I began to quickly and frequently see orbs in random photos. I feel strongly that these were/are signs of Boo Boo's presence, along with angelic beings guiding her. This instilled in me the belief that she continues to exist in another form and that we will someday reunite. This connection provided a much-needed anchor, giving me a sense of hope and continuity amidst the profound loss and physical pain.

Black spots — Early orbs in my backyard. I didn't know it at the time but I believe the black mark is Boo Boo's soul.

My assistant Dominique has also been privy to these extraordinary experiences, likely because his consciousness is attuned to mine. This connection seems crucial for perceiving these phenomena, suggesting that a shared consciousness might be vital to witnessing these remarkable sights.

While living on Earth, animals have a clear purpose: to be companions and to fulfill specific roles alongside us. However, their journey is not just limited to their time with us here; they, too, go through cycles of reincarnation. In this process, they evolve and progress, possibly to the point where they can attain a human form in their future incarnations. This idea has given me a new perspective on animals' significance and spiritual journey.

Boo Boo's influence extended well beyond her time on Earth. Her death led me to explore the interconnectedness of all life, the power of love, and the journey beyond the physical world. It has been a personal path filled with new truths and the comforting belief in unbreakable bonds of affection. Through this journey, I have not only paid tribute to Boo Boo's memory but also found a deeper sense of purpose and connection with the broader universe.

I immersed myself in a comprehensive process of learning and exploration. Through regular meditation sessions, thoughtful discussions with individuals well-versed in spiritual and philosophical disciplines, and significant time spent reading a wide range of materials, I began to question and reevaluate the conventional beliefs I once held.

This process allowed me to gain a deeper insight into life's nature, energy dynamics, and the concept of the soul's persistence beyond physical existence.

The loss of Boo Boo marked a crucial turning point in my life, serving as the catalyst for a profound period of introspection and revelation that significantly altered how I perceive the world. This period of transformation was not just about acquiring new knowledge; it was an experiential journey that gave me a clearer understanding of life's impermanent nature and the enduring significance of the connections we forge.

Through this exploration, I came to appreciate the intricate ways all aspects of the universe are intertwined. The relationship I shared with Boo Boo, which continued to resonate with me even after her passing, became a key factor in deepening my understanding of these universal connections. It highlighted how bonds formed in love and companionship can transcend the physical realm and offer gateways to broader spiritual insights.

I consider myself an ordinary guy. My life is filled with simple pleasures like playing poker, boating, and spending time with my wife, daughters, and grandkids. I never thought I was destined for anything beyond the typical, embodying the everyman in every sense. When I read *Walden* by Henry David Thoreau, a quote resonated with me: "The mass of men lead lives of quiet desperation." Perhaps my journey feels so liberating, removing any sense of desperation.

My transformation wasn't because I was extraordinary or had a background steeped in mysticism. I was just a regular guy who faced profound loss when my beloved dog passed away. This loss, however, became a turning point for me, awakening a greater purpose guided by spiritual beings.

This experience has taught me that profound spiritual encounters aren't reserved for the special few. Ordinary people living ordinary lives can experience the extraordinary. You don't need a monastic life to witness miracles or receive divine responses; these experiences are accessible to everyone and rooted in universal love.

Amateur Photographer

My everyday life began to follow a structured pattern, balancing ordinary tasks with my unique nighttime pursuit of connecting to the other world. Today, my day typically starts with activities that keep me grounded and connected to my surroundings. Although I still work, I always set aside time for meditation, which helps center my thoughts and emotions. After dinner, I take care of my new dogs, an everyday ritual that provides nourishment and a moment of pause. Attending to their needs and enjoying the companionship they offer is a source of great joy for me.

After completing mundane daily tasks, I venture outside, where, through photography and videography, I establish a connection with the spiritual realm. It's a time when I actively engage with and thank the entities from the other side, recognizing their existence and the wisdom they share. To ensure this exchange is safe and respectful, I adhere to certain rituals that help open and close the portals between our world and theirs. I discuss portals in greater detail in Chapter 6. These practices are vital for facilitating a harmonious interaction between the two realms.

This blend of mundane and spiritual practices defines my daily life, creating a grounding and transcendent rhythm. Through my photography, I capture images and engage in a deeper exploration of the world beyond, fostering a connection that enriches my understanding and appreciation of the universe's unseen aspects.

Upon closer inspection of these videos and images, I have observed phenomena that seemed like Boo Boo merging with or being transported by the orbs, with her face appearing in several captures. These experiences, where it felt like Boo Boo and other friendly presences were being visually represented through the orbs, provided me with a profound sense of her continued existence and closeness.

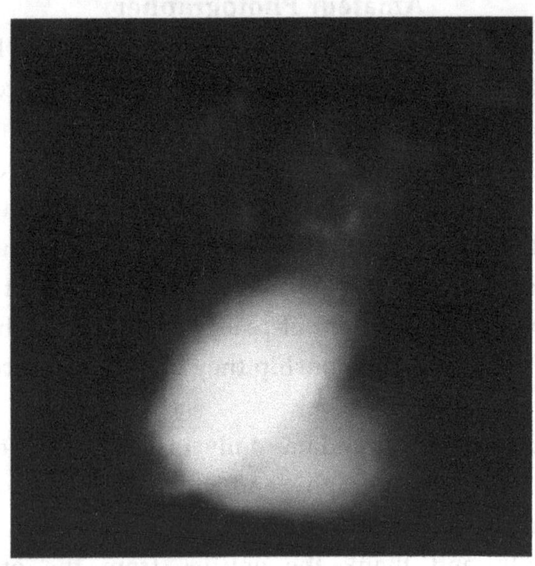

Do you see Boo Boo's face?

This newfound connection and the practice of capturing these moments nightly became a source of fascination and comfort, embedding the belief in my heart that Boo Boo's spirit is still with me, guiding me along my spiritual path.

I dedicate myself to my photography and videography practice, regardless of challenging weather conditions like biting cold, pitch darkness, or intense heat. Handling my equipment outdoors can be awkward and cumbersome at times. Still, I persist because this practice lifts the veil to spiritual entities. The responses I get through the images and footage I capture often convey messages of love and a deep-seated desire for our well-being, suggesting that there's more to this practice than meets the eye. This ongoing interaction provides a unique insight into the unseen world, reinforcing my commitment to braving any external conditions to capture these meaningful moments.

Although I wish these images could be viewed in three-dimensional detail, my current technology limits me to a more straightforward presentation. Intriguingly, when I pause these visuals, the scenes change, revealing different aspects or entities, suggesting a dynamic and interactive spiritual environment. While occasional darker elements appear, they never overshadow the protective presence of the sacred beings.

These visions consistently reveal divine or heavenly light, and I witness the presence of angels, archangels, seraphim (discussed in Chapter 6), and exotic animals. They depict an active portal, attracting souls that are overseen by a celestial hierarchy, including archangels and symbolic figures like a lion and a bear. Each vision is assisted by beings facilitating this spiritual journey, ensuring continuous guidance and protection.

I learned that the ambient light from nearby houses enhanced the clarity and vividness of the orbs in my photographs. Upon turning on the camera, vibrant orbs would sometimes appear right before it, leading to some of the most colorful images I've captured. Over four and a half years, I devoted myself to this passion, spending about 90% of my nights outside with my camera each year.

Working with a small monitor on my camera, I could only sometimes discern the details of what I was capturing once I reviewed the footage the following day. Occasionally, what was a significant capture in the viewfinder turned out unremarkable upon closer inspection. Yet, there were moments when the content was genuinely astonishing.

Sharing these discoveries was challenging. My assistant Dominique was one of the few people I could discuss my findings with, and even he was sometimes skeptical. Despite my enthusiasm, finding others who shared my interest or had the time to engage deeply with what I was trying to explain to them took a lot of work. Inviting someone to join me in capturing images of orbs was something only a handful of people would readily embrace.

The Sleeping Prophet

Edgar Cayce, known as the "Sleeping Prophet," was a prominent figure in the realms of spirituality, mysticism, and alternative medicine in America. Born on March 18, 1877, in Hopkinsville, Kentucky, Cayce demonstrated psychic abilities early in his life, with claims of seeing and communicating with spirits and having visions about his future.

Cayce's standout talent was his ability to enter a trance-like state, where he could tap into a broad spectrum of knowledge and insights, setting him apart in his field. In these states, he addressed questions on various subjects, including health, astrology, reincarnation, and other spiritual topics. These sessions, referred to as "readings," were recorded by his secretary and have been carefully preserved.

His approach to health was particularly forward-thinking, combining physical, mental, and spiritual well-being in a way ahead of his time. Cayce's advice often encompassed dietary adjustments, natural remedies, and mind-body techniques, many of which have since found support in contemporary alternative medicine.

In spirituality, Cayce's work touched on topics like the Akashic Records — a conceptual storehouse of universal knowledge encompassing the past, present, and future. I discuss Akashic Records in greater detail in Chapter 10. His readings explored Jesus' life and philosophies, the dynamics of karma and reincarnation, and even the lost civilization of Atlantis.

Despite his significant influence, Cayce remained modest about his abilities, often grappling with the implications of his talents. He established the Association for Research and Enlightenment (A.R.E.) in Virginia Beach to continue the exploration and sharing of his insights.

Edgar Cayce on Angels, Archangels, and the Unseen Forces is an insightful book that delves into and interprets Cayce's various teachings and readings, focusing on spiritual entities and broader metaphysical concepts. This compilation offers a deep dive into Cayce's perspectives on angels, archangels, and other intangible forces influencing our world and spiritual paths.

This book holds a special place in my spiritual journey. It connects me to the profound insights of a man renowned for his psychic abilities and deep spiritual understanding. Through Cayce's interpretations of the unseen and his explorations into the nature of these higher beings, I've found valuable guidance and a sense of connection to a larger, spiritual universe.

The teachings in this book resonate with me personally, offering clarity and direction in my exploration of spirituality. They help frame my experiences and curiosities within an expansive context grounded in Cayce's well-documented readings. Engaging with this material has enriched my understanding of the spiritual world. It has provided me with tools and perspectives to navigate my own spiritual path with more confidence and insight.

Below are some of the main points about the other side of the spiritual realm, as discussed in Cayce's book:

1. **Existence of Various Spiritual Beings:** Cayce's readings often reference many spiritual beings, including angels, archangels, and other entities. These beings exist in a realm not typically perceptible to the human physical senses, often referred to as the "other side" or the spiritual realm.
2. **Roles and Purposes of Angels and Archangels:** The book delves into these spiritual beings' specific roles and functions. Angels are often depicted as messengers or guides, assisting individuals in their spiritual journeys, and offering protection and guidance. Archangels are described as higher-ranking angels with more significant responsibilities, overseeing the realms of angels and interacting with humanity in profound ways.
3. **Interconnectedness of All Life:** Cayce emphasized the interconnectedness of all life, both physical and spiritual. This interconnectedness suggests that actions and thoughts on the physical plane can impact the spiritual realm and vice versa, illustrating a complex relationship between humans and spiritual entities.
4. **Spiritual Growth and Evolution:** The spiritual realm is also a place of growth and evolution for souls. Cayce's readings often discuss the concept of reincarnation and the soul's journey through various lifetimes, with the other side serving as a realm where souls review their past lives, learn from their experiences, and prepare for future incarnations.
5. **Unseen Forces:** In addition to angels and archangels, Cayce also discusses various unseen forces in the universe. These can include energetic influences, thought forms, and other nonphysical elements impacting individuals

and the world. A thought takes shape and becomes a form as (or while) we mentally or emotionally dwell upon it. Cayce perceived thoughts as so important that in 23 readings, he insisted that mental activity could be "miracles or crimes in action."

6. **Personal Guidance and Development:** Cayce believed individuals can receive guidance and insight from these spiritual beings and forces. Through meditation, prayer, and attunement to higher consciousness, people can connect with the other side for personal development, healing, and understanding of their life's purpose.

My Encounter with the Blessed Mother

I've had many transformative spiritual experiences (TSE). One time, inspired by my uncovering of the statue of the Healing Mary, I felt a strong desire to see the Blessed Mother in my video. After meditating and asking for her presence with sincere intent, I went about my day, which included a trip to Kroger Supermarket for groceries.

There, I encountered a woman with a young child, both barefoot, which was odd. She was pushing around an empty cart, which also was odd. The woman, who wore a cross around her neck, radiated an ethereal beauty and had dark black hair. She walked towards me and asked if I could help her buy baby formula. She must have had a baby at home, I thought to myself. I gave her $20, but she said it was $149. I remembered reading about how baby formula prices had skyrocketed, so I gave her all my money. She put her hands together as if praying and bowed her head to me. Her grateful reaction elicited an electric shock that went through me.

Feeling compelled to help further, I went to my car to get my checkbook to give her more money, but when I returned, she was nowhere to be found. No one else in the store remembered seeing her. I started tearing up because it struck me then that this encounter might have answered my prayer, a manifestation of the Blessed Mother, either through this woman or it was actually her. It was a powerful reminder of the importance of love and charity, values cherished by the Blessed Mother. Although I never saw the woman or child again, the experience left a lasting impact on me, reinforcing the significance of kindness and giving in our lives.

Questions & Answers

Q: Is there a relationship between science and spirituality?

A: I love this question because I believe there is a relationship. I have done a lot of reading about quantum physics, and the intersection of quantum physics and divinity is fascinating to me. The key point here is that these realms are not mutually exclusive. In fact, they are interconnected, suggesting that there is a singular divine force orchestrating the vast complexity of the universe. This force encompasses a hierarchy that includes various spiritual beings like archangels, seraphim, cherubim, and others, illustrating the expansive nature of the universe and its spiritual dimensions.

Q: What books should the reader start with to help them with their journey?

A: I understand the challenge given the sheer number of books you have already likely encountered. It's important to select titles that align with your current level of understanding and curiosity. Since you might be new to exploring these concepts, I'll focus on books that are suitable for beginners on their spiritual journey. Starting with foundational texts will be beneficial. It's crucial to choose resources that lay a solid groundwork for understanding these complex topics. Please see my list of recommended reading at the end of this book.

Q: If someone else used a camera as powerful as yours, would they be able to see the same orbs?

A: Those who have tried to capture orbs in my yard with their cameras usually don't see what I do. It seems that seeing orbs isn't just about the camera's strength, but it's also about the viewer's intention and their ability to connect with these entities through love and kindness. While it's true that anyone can stumble upon orbs in random photos, having a genuine and pure intent seems crucial for a more meaningful interaction with them. For instance, I doubt that others would easily see my dog in their photos. When it comes to videos, numerous skilled photographers have tried and failed to record orbs or spirits in my yard, except for Dominique, who has recently succeeded in capturing spirits on video.

Q: Do you believe that personal circumstances affect what individuals perceive in orbs?

A: Yes, I do think that what people see in orbs can reflect their own life experiences. Orbs are present at all times, both day and night, and are frequently observed at emotionally significant events like weddings and graduations. However, many people overlook them, either because they're not actively searching for orbs or they dismiss them as mere lens flares or camera glitches when they do notice them.

Q: Do you think interpretations of orbs can vary, or is there a singular truth to what they represent, especially since you're the one calling forth the spirits?

A: When it comes to a standard round orb, there isn't much room for interpretation. The color represents a specific holy entity, and sometimes you can discern a person, spirit, or animal within it. For example, the orbs in Diana Cooper and Kathy Crosswell's book, *Ascension Through Orbs*, appear the same to everyone, whether they actively seek them or not. These orbs often manifest due to a subconscious desire or because a spiritual being or a departed loved one is present during joyful events like weddings or graduations. However, the videos I record are different. They don't just show standard orbs; they display projections from spiritual beings that respond to my meditations and subconscious requests. These projections are meant to aid my spiritual growth or provide comfort. Since they're 3D, people might see different things based on their perspective and proximity to the video or image. But, since I'm the one directly interacting with these entities, my interpretation of the videos is likely the most accurate.

Q: What exactly are we observing in these images? Are they visuals from a spiritual realm, selectively shown through an orb? Could they be glimpses of heaven? And who are these unearthly beings appearing in almost every video, seemingly guiding animal souls?

A: I believe I can shed some light on these inquiries while also identifying the angels and sacred entities that appear in my videos. This raises an even broader question: when people recount near-death experiences (NDEs) involving encounters with divine beings or visions of heaven, how can we be certain of what they've witnessed? They rely on their memories, but can we confirm it was heaven they experienced? While I trust their accounts, I have videos that support my own interpretations and provide tangible evidence of these spiritual encounters.

In concluding this chapter, we reflect on the journey from a singular, compelling encounter with a green orb to a broader quest for understanding and meaning within the realm of the unseen. This narrative is not just a chronicle of personal discovery; it's an invitation to my readers to embark on your own explorations, to question the nature of your reality, and be open to possibilities beyond the conventional boundaries of perception.

The journey from essential photography tools to more sophisticated equipment signifies a deeper commitment to uncovering the truths hidden in plain sight, illustrating the evolution from casual observer to dedicated investigator. Each orb captured, each image analyzed, adds a piece to the puzzle, offering glimpses into a largely unexplored and mysterious dimension.

We must acknowledge that the quest to understand orbs and their implications is ongoing. The interpretations and insights gained thus far are stepping stones in a vast, uncharted territory. The green orb seen above Boo Boo's head was not just an anomaly; it was a gateway, opening avenues for exploration and introspection.

This narrative serves as a testament to the curiosity that drives us, the unseen forces that intrigue us, and the endless pursuit of knowledge that defines our existence. As we move forward, let us carry the lesson that the world is filled with wonders waiting to be understood. Our innate curiosity will lead us to unveil the mysteries of the universe, one orb at a time.

Chapter 5
Experts Weigh In

The illiterate of the 21st century will not be those who cannot read and write, but those who cannot learn, unlearn, and relearn.

Alvin Toffler

In this chapter, I aim to provide a balanced and respectful overview of the various perspectives on orbs, acknowledging the rich spiritual beliefs surrounding them and the scientific explanations that challenge these interpretations. I encourage a holistic view that remains open to the mystery and wonder of orbs, whether seen as spiritual phenomena, optical effects, or phenomena yet to be fully understood by either domain.

The Allure of the Orb

Orbs, essentially spheres of light, have consistently intrigued people due to their mysterious nature. They appear in different colors and sizes, and are found in various settings. Often linked with supernatural phenomena, orbs exist in a space that is not fully understood, balancing between scientific explanation and the unexplained. This chapter explores various aspects of orbs, including their physical characteristics, the range of theories proposed to explain them, and the vast array of beliefs and interpretations they have sparked across cultures and individuals. With their glowing appearance, these orbs have been reported in many places and under various conditions. They can be small and subtle, or large and bright, and their colors can range from white to blue to other hues. This diversity in appearance has led to many questions about what orbs really are and why they appear the way they do.

Three orbs in my neighbor's yard. If you look closely, you can see Boo Boo's face in the two larger ones.

The theories about orbs are as varied as their appearances. Some people believe orbs are natural phenomena, such as reflections of light or particles in the air illuminated in a certain way. Others think they might be evidence of paranormal activity, such as the presence of spirits or other entities beyond our usual sensory perception. These theories often blend scientific inquiry and a desire to understand the unknown.

Alongside these theories, orbs have inspired various beliefs and interpretations. In some cultures, they are seen as omens or messages from the spirit world. In others, they are viewed as a natural part of the environment, no more mysterious than rain or sunlight. The interpretation of orbs often depends on the individual's beliefs, cultural background, and experiences.

In summary, this exploration of orbs is not just an investigation into a specific type of phenomenon. It's a journey through how people interpret the world around them, combining observable facts with unexplained mysteries. By examining orbs from multiple perspectives, we can better understand both the phenomenon itself and the various ways humans seek to make sense of the unexplained aspects of their world.

Echoes of the Past

Orbs' history is deeply intertwined with ancient mythologies and various cultures worldwide. These orbs have been perceived and interpreted in different societies in numerous ways. For example, in Greek mythology, orbs are often mentioned as vehicles or conveyors used by gods and goddesses. They were seen as a means for divine beings to travel or communicate with humans.

In the traditions of indigenous peoples, orbs are viewed quite differently. They are often considered sacred symbols, representing the presence or messages of ancestral spirits. In these cultures, orbs are not just natural phenomena but are deeply connected with spiritual beliefs and practices.

Throughout history, these interpretations of orbs have found their way into various art forms. They have been depicted in paintings, sculptures, and other artistic expressions, illustrating how different cultures envisioned them. Similarly, orbs have been mentioned and revered in numerous texts, including religious scriptures, folklore, and historical accounts. This shows that orbs have always been a subject of human fascination and curiosity.

This fascination continues in modern times. Orbs still capture the imagination of people across the world. They are discussed in the context of both historical beliefs and contemporary experiences. Whether seen as mystical signs, spiritual messengers, or simply unexplained natural occurrences, orbs remain a topic of interest and speculation. Their presence in ancient mythologies and cultures highlights humanity's long-standing interest in the mysterious and the unexplained, a curiosity that persists today.

The Art of Orb Photography

Capturing images of orbs has developed into a specific skill and hobby, driven largely by a mix of fascination and personal belief. Those who are enthusiastic about this, including myself, often use cameras that are adjusted to be highly sensitive to capture these elusive orbs. This pursuit typically takes place in low-light conditions or at night, when these mysterious spheres are believed to be more visible.

In terms of visual appearance, orbs show up as round, glowing shapes in our photographs and videos. They can vary significantly in size, appearing as tiny dots or larger, more noticeable objects. The colors of these orbs are also varied, with some being almost transparent while others display bright, multiple colors. Although cameras often capture these orbs, which might seem to move in a way that's hard to catch, some people say they have seen orbs moving even without a camera or video recorder.

The way orbs seem to move or float in the air, often described as a kind of dance, adds to their mystique. Eyewitness accounts vary, with some describing slow, drifting motions, and others talking about quick, darting movements.

Whether appearing as faint glimmers or distinct, colorful spheres, they capture the attention of casual observers and those more deeply interested in their potential meanings and origins.

Some orb enthusiasts, myself included, even claim to have a natural ability to attract these orbs. In my experience, taking photos of orbs becomes more than just pointing and shooting; it's like interacting with unseen forces. We can encourage these orbs to appear and be captured on camera through certain techniques or personal abilities.

In Chapter 6, I delve deeper into this topic. I will discuss the concept of portals – a term some in the paranormal community use to describe gateways to other realms or dimensions. I will explore the idea that it's possible to learn techniques to create these portals or to enhance one's natural ability to interact with them. This chapter will provide insight into how some people believe they can actively engage with and capture these orbs, transforming photography into a more interactive and mystical experience.

Science Decodes

In scientific terms, orbs are frequently explained as the result of ordinary, everyday occurrences related to how light interacts with its surroundings. They are often seen as the product of light interacting with small particles such as dust or moisture in the air. When light hits these particles, it can refract or scatter, creating bright circular shapes that we see as orbs in photos or videos.

Camera equipment also plays a significant role in the appearance of orbs. Lens flares, when a light source shines directly into the lens, can create bright spots or circles resembling orbs. Additionally, the way digital cameras process images can sometimes inadvertently produce these orb-like shapes. This is especially true in low-light conditions, where the camera's sensor might struggle to capture the scene accurately, leading to visual artifacts that can be mistaken for orbs.

These explanations categorize orbs as unintended byproducts of modern photography and videography. From this perspective, the bright circles that many interpret as supernatural or otherworldly are simply the result of how cameras and their lenses capture and process light under certain conditions. What might seem mysterious or paranormal at first glance can often be attributed to the more mundane workings of optics and camera technology.

As such, this world is not without its dissenters. Skeptical critics challenge the orb's mystique, arguing for a grounded interpretation rooted in photography's quirks. They call for a return to critical thinking, urging a scientific exploration free from the lure of the supernatural.

The simple debate over orbs' existence and nature is ongoing. According to Rick Moran, coordinator for the Association for the Study of Unexplained Phenomenon, Inc., "While orbs have fascinated ghost hunters, especially in the digital photography era, they often result from camera design rather than otherworldly origins. It's essential in paranormal research to critically analyze photographs, considering factors like camera quality, lens filters, and environmental conditions."

Beyond the Tangible

Moving past the scientific explanations, there's a different perspective where orbs take on a supernatural significance. In paranormal investigation and belief, orbs are often seen as more than just simple light reflections or camera glitches. Many interested in the paranormal view orbs as manifestations of spiritual energy or indicators of a ghostly presence. This is particularly true in places famous for being haunted or having a rich history of ghost stories.

In these settings, orbs are not dismissed as trivial or accidental. Instead, they are considered important signs, potentially representing the presence of spirits or other entities from beyond the physical world. For those who believe in the paranormal, these orbs serve as a silent witness to activities or presences that are not perceivable through ordinary means. They are seen as a form of connection or communication from realms that we, as humans, need to fully understand or have the ability to directly interact with.

Perspectives Around the Globe

Throughout my journey, I have often sought the teachings of Diana Cooper. I highly recommend her books, some of which she has coauthored with Kathy Crosswell. In their book *Ascension Through Orbs,* Cooper and Crosswell focus on the belief that orbs are spiritual beings or energy manifestations that can assist individuals in their spiritual growth and ascension process.

Orbs as spiritual beings: The belief that orbs are not merely dust particles or camera anomalies but spiritual beings or energy forms that carry divine consciousness and messages.
Divine guidance and support: Orbs are seen as messengers from higher realms, offering guidance, protection, and support to individuals on their spiritual journey.
Ascension activation: Orbs are believed to have the power to activate and accelerate the process of spiritual awakening and ascension, helping individuals raise their vibration and expand their consciousness.
Healing and transformation: Orbs are seen as carriers of healing energy, assisting in the clearing and balancing of energetic blockages and facilitating emotional, mental, and physical healing.
Connection with higher realms: Orbs are considered a means of connecting with higher-dimensional beings, such as angels, spirit guides, and ascended masters, fostering a deeper connection with the spiritual realms.
Conscious photography and meditation: Ascension through orbs often involves conscious photography, where individuals intentionally capture orb images and meditation techniques to connect with the orb's energy and receive its messages. "Orbs respond to the consciousness of the photographer. If your heart is open and you resonate at a fifth-dimension frequency, you can take orb photographs," state Cooper and Crosswell.

Another book I recommend is *Orbs: Their Mission and Messages of Hope* by Klaus Heinemann, Ph.D., and Gundi Heinemann. Klaus was a researcher previously affiliated with NASA. They provide a mesmerizing exploration of orbs. They expertly weave together the tapestry of worldwide ideas, beliefs, and experiences.

They provide a detailed examination of numerous photographs where orbs make their appearances. Klaus and Gundi Heinemann are not quick to dismiss these orbs as mere photographic flukes like dust particles or moisture. Instead, they have concluded that they are in the camp who believe that orbs are spiritual beings or energies. This interpretation paints a picture of a world where angels, spirit guides, or even entities from other dimensions brush against our reality, visible as orbs.

Personal stories and anecdotes add a human touch to their analysis. Various individuals share their encounters with orbs, painting a vivid picture of the personal and often deeply impactful experiences these sightings entail. These accounts lend weight to the idea that orbs are not mere visual specters but entities with a meaningful presence.

An intriguing aspect of their research is the connection between orbs, human consciousness, and intention. The Heinemanns propose a thought-provoking theory: the appearance of orbs might be linked to our emotional or spiritual states. This notion suggests a fascinating intertwining of our inner lives with these mysterious phenomena.

At the core of the book is a message of hope and transformation. The Heinemanns see orbs as beacons of a higher spiritual reality, bringing messages that inspire reflection, spiritual growth, and transformation. It's a vision of orbs as catalysts, encouraging us to ponder our lives and spiritual journeys.

While embracing the spiritual, the Heinemanns also acknowledge the scientific and skeptical viewpoints regarding orbs. They present a balanced view, though their narrative favors the spiritual interpretation.

Lastly, the Heinemanns delve into the technical aspects of capturing these elusive orbs on camera. They discuss photographic techniques and analyze various conditions and settings that might influence the appearance of orbs, providing a comprehensive look at the mystical and practical aspects of orb photography.

Michael Newton, Ph.D., has made significant contributions to this field with his research on reincarnation and life between lives. He wrote two volumes of his studies called *Journey of Souls*. His work delves into the spiritual journey of souls, using hypnotic regression to uncover insights into the afterlife. According to Newton, the progression of souls can be seen through a spectrum of colors, echoing the beliefs about orb colors.

UK spiritual advisor and medium Rachel Keene takes a methodical and rational approach when investigating orbs. Her methodology involves first ruling out common, mundane explanations for orbs in photos or videos. Keene's extensive experience is rooted in her visits to hundreds of locations and analyses of thousands of images. She maintains that once everyday factors like moisture, dust, and other typical environmental elements are discounted, the presence of orbs in images could indicate spirit energy.

Keene explains that in instances where a photo is taken shortly after someone has walked through an area, especially in a dusty environment, or where there are small insects, pet hair, or any movement near the camera, likely, what is captured is merely particles close to the lens. However, if such ordinary physical causes are meticulously ruled out, the orbs observed might have a more intriguing origin.

According to Keene, genuine spirit orbs often exhibit distinct patterns, a nucleus-like center, and sometimes even shapes resembling faces. However, these are not actual faces of spirits. This is due to humans' innate tendency to find familiar patterns, such as faces, in random shapes, a phenomenon known as pareidolia. During a paranormal investigation in a haunted pub, Keene cites an instance where what she considers a real orb was captured on a digital camera.

Keene also notes that orbs are sometimes seen in photographs alongside mists or smoky shapes, which differ from the orbs. These mists can occasionally form shapes that represent the spirit manifesting itself. She recounts a specific case from 2003, where a photograph captured in an area with a rich indigenous history showed the unmistakable face of an elder in the mist, believed to be a benign family protector.

In Keene's view, actual spirit orbs and other light anomalies are physical reactions to the energy expended when a spirit manifests, akin to exhaust produced by a vehicle as a byproduct of combustion. She cites Newton's third law of motion that for every action there is an equal and opposite reaction, so when a spirit expends energy to manifest in our physical world, it produces orbs and other phenomena. This manifestation requires a significant amount of energy from a spirit. It can lead to various effects, such as orbs, mists, temperature changes, sudden breezes, unexplained noises, or lights.

Keene further explains that everything, whether alive, deceased, or inanimate, operates at a specific vibrational speed in line with the laws of physics. From her experiences as a medium, she has observed that when the physical body dies, consciousness continues in another state, with all memories, personality traits, and intelligence intact. She believes the spirit world, or the place between lives, exists alongside our physical world but at a different vibrational speed.

She also notes that while spirits do not have a physical form, they can inhabit one and exist outside of it, as evidenced by out-of-body and near-death experiences. Keene's belief in life after death is supported by the scientific principle that energy does not cease to exist; it simply changes form.

Keene mentions that when communicating with spirits, they often present themselves as remembered in the physical world. This allows mediums like her to describe their appearance, personality, ailments, how they died, and their life experiences. Since spirits no longer inhabit the physical plane, they recreate these appearances based on their memories for communicative purposes.

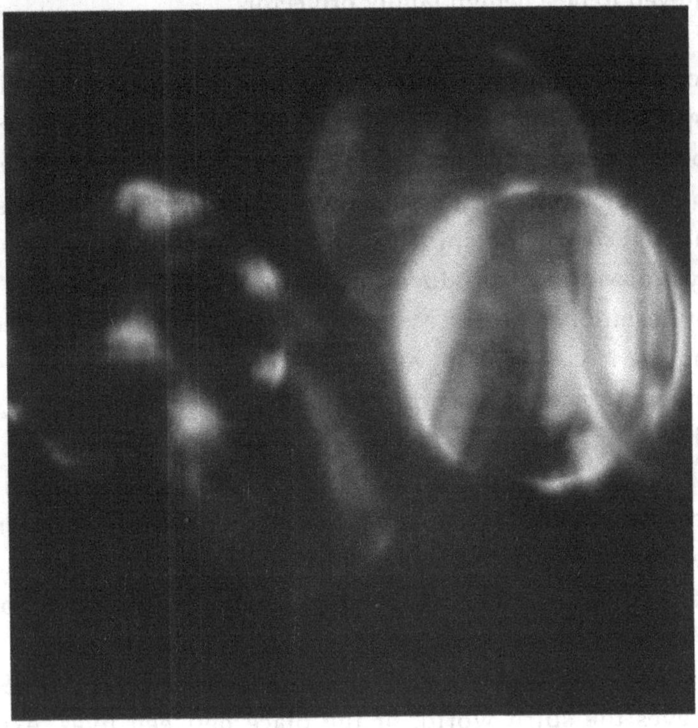

LOTS going on! There are multiple orbs. On the left are six midway creatures. In the upper middle is an unknown entity. In the right orb is my guardian angel looking back.

A Spiritual Healer's Retreat

In a fascinating case, a gentleman named Merryn Jose took several photographs during a gathering of spiritual healers. Also, there was Klaus Heinemann who noticed something unusual in these images: a recurring pale, moon-like circle of light. Initially, Heinemann, who brought a skeptical and scientific viewpoint, thought these circles were simply errors in the photography. However, as he, himself, continued to take more photographs, especially at spiritual events, he began to see a pattern that was hard to dismiss. These "orbs," as they came to be known, seemed to appear in photographs specifically when requested, which left Heinemann perplexed.

Heinemann's professional background in microscopic techniques and optical resolution lent significant credibility to his detailed investigation. Despite conducting rigorous tests, including experiments using two cameras simultaneously, these orbs showed up unpredictably. This inconsistency in their appearance suggested that they might not always be visible, leading Heinemann to consider the possibility of a paranormal element in these occurrences.

The characteristics of these orbs, like their ability to move quickly and appear selectively in photographs, fascinated Heinemann and other scientific minds. At a conference in Sedona, Arizona, dedicated experts gathered to discuss the potentially paranormal nature of these orbs. The meeting underscored the idea that phenomena could still be legitimate subjects for scientific inquiry even if not yet proven.

Several notable figures, including physicist and clairvoyant, William Tiller, and Professor of Systematic Theology, Miceal Ledwith, offered their perspectives. They likened the mystery surrounding orbs to groundbreaking discoveries in the history of science. Tiller pointed out the limitations of human vision in understanding the full spectrum of reality. At the same time,

Ledwith drew comparisons with early misconceptions about the existence of bacteria.

Adding another layer to this mystery were the experiences of photographer Anna Donaldson, who encountered orbs while taking photos with medium Keith Watson. Her experiences suggested a potential connection between these orbs and spiritual entities. Despite the skepticism surrounding such claims, the consistent appearance of orbs under various conditions provoked thought and debate about their true nature.

Nicholas McGirr, known for his ghost tours in the historic streets of Charleston, offered a perspective that reflects the complexity of interpreting such phenomena: "We are raised in a society where we are taught to believe a more logical reason for an illogical happening rather than the illogical reason for something which may be of the unknown, hence, why the logical answer is illogical to the logical person." On his tours, McGirr encourages participants to take multiple photos of the same scene to confirm or debunk any unusual occurrences captured in the images.

Interpreting Orb Colors

The different colors of orbs are thought to signify varying aspects or moods of a spirit. Here's a simplified interpretation of various orb colors:

- **Clear:** Signifies communicative energy
- **Black/Brown:** Indicates a potentially unsafe area
- **Red/Orange:** Symbolizes safety and security
- **Green:** Represents a human spirit or a connection with nature
- **Blue:** Associated with psychic energy or truth
- **Gray:** Suggests the presence of fear
- **Pink:** Denotes love

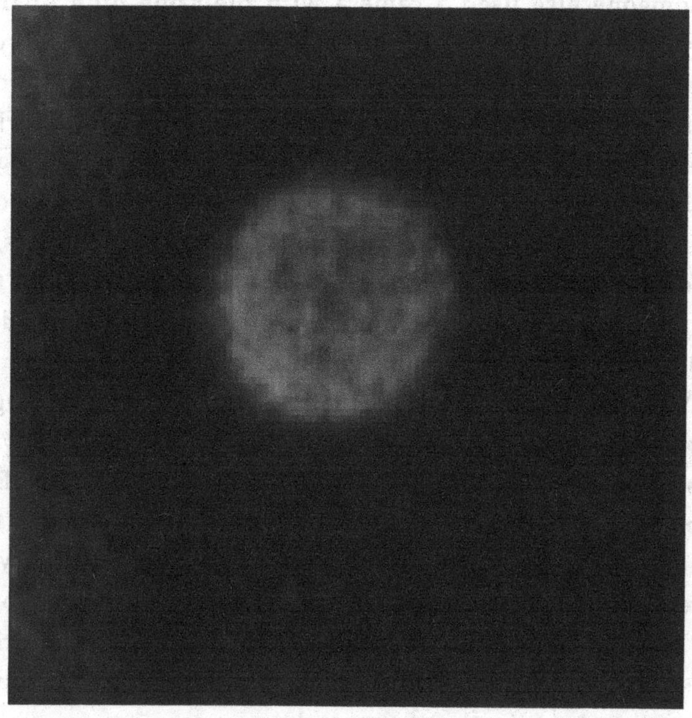

Orb holding Boo Boo.

My Perspective

This has been quite an educational and spiritual journey. Early on, I realized that I am a mere vessel in which to teach others. This knowledge gives me great joy; it literally makes me smile. I am so happy to be on this path of awakening and enlightenment. I will rejoice in fulfilling my destiny if I can help even one person as they seek their truth.

People often ask me about the practical research I conduct in my backyard because I have hundreds of hours of video-capturing orbs and the spirit guides and angels within. I want to share some of the more common questions I receive and provide my answers here:

If someone else used a camera with the same high quality as yours, would they capture the same orb images? From what I've seen, others who have tried using equally advanced cameras have yet to be able to replicate my success in capturing these orbs. This ties in with the ideas presented by Diana Cooper and Kathy Crosswell, who suggest that a conscious connection, driven by pure intentions of love and kindness, is necessary to truly "see" or capture orbs. It's not just about the technical capability of the camera but also about the mindset and intentions of the person using it.

Yes, anyone can indeed take random photos where orbs might appear. However, having pure intent matters significantly in this context. For instance, I often see an orb I refer to as Boo Boo, but I'm pretty skeptical that others would see her in the same way I do. This belief is reinforced by my experiences with several skilled photographers who have tried but have yet to do so. This, again, suggests to me that there's more to capturing these orbs than just pointing a camera and shooting. It involves a deeper, more intentional approach.

Suppose other people observe some form of activity or presence within orbs. Is it likely that they are witnessing the same angels or archangels that you perceive? Based on my experiences and beliefs, they are not. The specific angels and archangels that appear to me through these orbs are unique to my personal experience. They are present for a reason – to guide, teach, and offer support specific to my needs and questions on my spiritual journey.

I don't see these beings as random or wandering entities that appear indiscriminately to anyone. Instead, they have a purposeful connection to me and my spiritual path. When I encounter these angels or archangels within the orbs, it feels like they are responding to my queries or providing assistance tailored to my circumstances.

This perspective might imply that everyone's experience with orbs could be unique and deeply personal. The entities or energies others perceive in orbs could be different, potentially aligning with their spiritual needs or journeys. These orbs act as a personal and direct channel of communication or interaction with the spiritual realm, varying from person to person based on their individual paths and requirements.

Do you believe that what individuals perceive within orbs is influenced by their personal experiences and what's happening? My answer is yes. Orbs are everywhere, both during the day and at night. These orbs, which I consider to be spiritually guided entities, often appear at emotionally significant events like weddings, graduations, and other gatherings filled with inspiration and love.

The critical point here is that while these orbs are present, many people either need to actively look for them or be unaware of their significance. As a result, when someone notices an orb, especially in a photograph, their first instinct is to dismiss it as a camera lens flare or just a quirk of the lighting rather than considering it might be something more. People might be surrounded by orbs at poignant moments in their lives. Yet, they may not realize it because they aren't expecting to see such phenomena or don't recognize them when they appear.

This perception, or lack thereof, of orbs can be closely linked to what is happening in a person's life. When someone is going through a significant moment or a period of emotional intensity, they might be more open to noticing these orbs or the orbs might appear more frequently. However, the general lack of awareness or understanding about orbs means that they often need to be recognized and understood even when they are present.

Do you have a more accurate understanding since you have facilitated the spirits' presence? If the orb in a photograph is just a regular, round shape, there's little room for varied interpretation. The orb's color often represents the nature of the spirit within it, and sometimes it's possible to discern a figure, be it a person, spirit, or animal. For instance, in Diana Cooper and Kathy Crosswell's book, the orbs depicted look the same to every viewer. They appear either in response to a subconscious request or as a manifestation of a holy entity or a departed relative, particularly during times of joy and happiness.

However, the orbs that I capture in my videos are different. They aren't just standard orbs; they are specific projections directed by a holy entity in response to my subconscious requests and meditations. Sometimes, they impart a lesson, aid my personal growth, or provide comfort.

Given that these orbs manifest in response to my specific "call," I believe my interpretation of what they represent is the most accurate. While others may see the same orb and perceive something differently, my close involvement in their emergence and understanding of their purpose lead me to trust my interpretations as the most reliable. The process of these orbs appearing is closely linked to my intentions and spiritual practices, which suggests that my perspective on what they signify is particularly well-informed.

Where can we see orbs? Orbs can be seen in many different environments but are most often observed in their full glory at night. Thanks to technological advancements, almost anyone with a camera or smartphone can capture images of these orbs. Yet, it requires more than a device to truly appreciate their captivating beauty, complex shapes, vibrant colors, and the deeper meanings they might represent. Engaging with orbs on a more profound level, through heightened awareness and emotional connection, enhances the experience.

The significance of orbs goes beyond being a visual spectacle; they are seen as vessels for holy beings, including angels, archangels, and even the spirits of departed humans and animals. These orbs are believed to move between different realms and sometimes visit our world. It's thought that the more a person tries to connect with orbs subconsciously, the more likely they are to attract and capture their images. This process of attracting and photographing orbs is made easier with the sensitive sensors in modern cameras and smartphones, which can record videos and images under various lighting conditions.

Is there a link between orbs and near-death experiences (NDEs)? I believe there is. People who have gone through NDEs often describe seeing orbs during their experiences, especially when they feel they are outside of their physical body. This observation leads to an interesting question: why aren't these orbs seen as being directly related to the person's physical body during such intense experiences? The explanation is how individuals perceive their surroundings during an NDE. Rather than observing from the outside, they may be experiencing a journey within the orb, entering a different aspect of reality.

People who report seeing orbs during NDEs describe them as having a significant impact on their experience. These orbs aren't just passive objects; they play an active role in the person's experience. The orbs could facilitate the soul's journey during these critical moments, providing guidance or transition from the physical world to other realms.

Furthermore, these experiences with orbs during NDEs challenge our conventional understanding of reality and the afterlife. They suggest that elements and processes at work in the universe are beyond our current scientific knowledge. In essence, orbs, as reported by individuals who have experienced NDEs, represent a fascinating intersection of the physical and the spiritual, offering a glimpse into the profound mysteries of life, death, and what may lie beyond.

What I Know So Far:

- Orbs are not explainable with conventional physics.
- They are emanations from intelligent life outside of the conventional physical realm.
- We must use discernment.
- They have different intensities (some require digital image enhancement).
- They can move extremely fast.
- They move in discrete steps.
- They have individualistic features and may have "faces."
- They appear to show with facial features primarily to those who are inclined to see them.
- They can follow instructions.
- They appear to be highly intelligent.
- They can expand (possibly to infinite size) and contract (possibly to atomic size) extremely fast.
- Their intelligence and ability to contract and expand at infinite speeds allow for the hypothesis that they may be instrumental in certain aspects of alternative/spiritual healing.
- Thought projections look similar to orbs.
- They appear to want to communicate to us through their appearance and location in photos.
- Their messages appear to be benevolent and helpful to individual people and mankind at large.
- In videos, they demonstrate that they can penetrate through walls and reappear at a different location.

In conclusion, I want to state that I believe there is more to orbs than just the effects of refracted light, dust particles, or any other simple explanation that skeptics often suggest. However, I recognize that there is still a lot of debate about what orbs actually are. People's opinions on orbs range widely, from those who are highly skeptical to others who, like me, believe strongly in their spiritual significance.

It's important to look at orbs critically and question them, which is a standard method in scientific research. But it's also crucial to realize that our understanding of phenomena like orbs is often shaped by societal norms that lean heavily towards logical and scientifically proven explanations, sometimes overlooking the possibility of things that are not yet understood or explained.

As we continue to study and learn about orbs, they represent an interesting overlap between science and what might be considered paranormal. This challenges us to reexamine what we believe to be accurate or possible. The mystery surrounding orbs keeps them a topic of scientific research and spiritual fascination. They are an area where the quest for factual evidence and the sense of wonder and spirituality intersects. We are all at a point where we have to balance what we believe and what we can prove, with each new piece of information leading us further into exploring these intriguing unknowns.

Huge orb with the energies of three archangels. This was a week after Boo Boo had passed and I believe they were checking in on me.

Chapter 6

Portals to the Other Side

Native American Legend says that the sky is a great dome and there is a hole in it through which the spirits pass in order to get to heaven.

Admiral William H. McRaven

I've always been fascinated by portals, not the digital kind we encounter through computers and emails, where we exchange files or meet in online groups, but something more mystical. My interest deepened after reading Diana Cooper's book *Birthing a New Civilization: Transition to the New Golden Age in 2032*. In her book, Cooper introduces the idea of creating portals, which she describes as openings or gateways that enhance spiritual growth, promote healing, and establish a deeper connection between our physical world and the higher spiritual realms. These portals are channels that allow a more powerful flow of spiritual energy, characterized by high frequencies, to permeate our environment. This influx of energy can support both individual growth and the collective advancement of the planet towards a higher state of being, a process often referred to as ascension.

Cooper's discussion on portals is part of a larger conversation about transitioning into a new era marked by greater spiritual awareness and awakening. She proposes that individuals can actively participate in this transition by creating portals themselves. The purpose behind establishing these portals is to channel love, and support the ascension of souls, facilitating their journey towards a higher, more peaceful existence, which she equates with the concept of heaven.

Cooper emphasizes the need for clear intention to create a portal. The process involves visualizing or imagining a gateway through which divine energy can flow freely into our world. This energy can uplift and heal not just individuals, but the planet as a whole. Creating a portal is a personal spiritual practice and a service to the broader community and the world, contributing to the collective shift towards a more enlightened and spiritually connected society.

This idea resonates strongly with me, and I wholeheartedly agree with this ideology. By focusing our intentions on our core values of love and healing, we effectively anchor these divine frequencies into our world, which not only assists individual growth but also has a ripple effect, contributing to the healing and upliftment of the planet.

This perspective is particularly compelling because it empowers us to play an active role in the spiritual awakening.

It emphasizes the power of individual actions guided by a collective intention toward love and positive transformation. Creating a portal becomes a deeply personal yet universally impactful practice, blending personal spiritual development with the broader mission of ushering in a "new age" of enlightenment and harmony.

Moreover, Cooper's approach aligns with my own belief that spirituality and the physical world are not separate but interconnected. By establishing these portals, we facilitate a flow of divine energy into our environment and affirm our commitment to being stewards of this planet and guardians of its spiritual evolution. It's a reminder that each of us holds the potential to effect meaningful change, both in our personal lives and on the broader world.

In embracing Cooper's teachings on portals, I see a clear path forward for anyone looking to deepen their spiritual practice and contribute to a collective shift towards a brighter, more enlightened future. It's a call to action that I agree with and am inspired by. It offers a concrete way to weave spirituality into daily life's fabric and participate in a global movement toward healing, love, and ascension. This approach, grounded in practicality yet soaring in its spiritual ambition, is a powerful testament to the role we can all play in crafting the new era of enlightenment that Diana Cooper so vividly envisions.

Seraphim Angels

Seraphim (a type of angel) and even mythical creatures like dragons play a role in guiding souls to ascension. They help in collecting the souls and transporting them to their next destination.

The process involves seraphim transports, essentially angelic beings tasked with moving souls across different realms, whether on Earth or other planets. This concept is like what some people describe as near-death experiences: a moment of darkness followed by traveling through a tunnel to a light and something beyond.

This tunnel to the light, and the journey it represents, is believed to be the path souls take as they are loaded onto these seraphim transports. It's a way of understanding how souls transition from our world to the next, guided by benevolent forces like seraphim and supported by the focused intentions and prayers of those who create portals.

Based on my video evidence, souls pass through the portal and are then collected by entities called "midwayers," operating under the supervision of seraphim, before being transferred onto seraphim transport vehicles. This process is visible and verifiable in the evidence I have. However, what remains uncertain in my research is the specific nature of the journey souls undertake after death, mainly through the tunnel of light. This journey often includes a phase where the deceased encounters a welcoming party of previously departed family and friends or a "soul family." In near-death experiences, individuals report meeting spiritual beings, such as deities or guardian angels, who show them various aspects of their existence and offer them a choice between staying in the afterlife or returning to the earthly plane.

During these encounters, the individual's life is reviewed, much like opening and examining a book that details their earthly experiences, assessing their actions and character. Following this review, if the individual concurs with the presented path, they progress to different levels of existence, referred to as "mansion worlds," where their soul's journey continues through stages, ideally moving toward a state of paradise.

Piecing it all together, the sequence I propose is that upon death, souls travel through the portal, are gathered by midwayers under the seraphim's oversight, and then board the seraphim transports to their next destination, likely the mansion worlds where they undergo life reviews and continue their spiritual progression. This sequence aligns with the evidence and the narrative presented in the book, *The Urantia Book: Revealing the Mysteries of God, the Universe, World History, Jesus, and Ourselves*, suggesting a structured process of soul transition and progression in the afterlife.

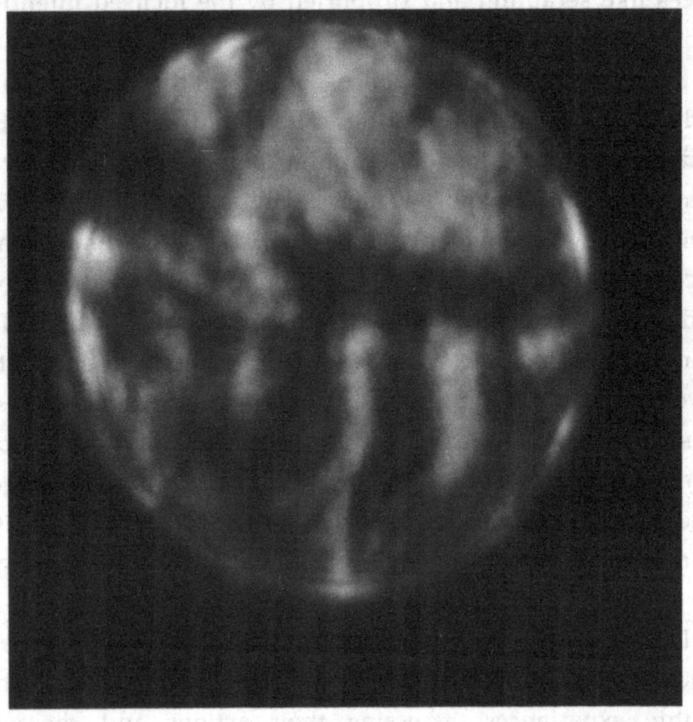

From left to right: a boy looking in wonder, Archangel Ariel, three midway creatures.

In the Bible, "seraphim" refers to a type of angelic being that's especially highlighted in the Old Testament, mainly in the book of Isaiah. Chapter six of Isaiah gives us a clear look into what is described as the divine throne room, showing us how these beings fit into the spiritual realm.

Isaiah's description of his encounter with the seraphim is one of the most detailed views of angels in the Bible. It shows us the structure of heaven's hierarchy and how worship works there. He describes the seraphim as magnificent beings with six wings: Two wings cover their faces out of respect for God, two cover their feet as a sign of humility, and the remaining two fly as they carry out their duties.

What makes the seraphim particularly interesting is how they look and their role in continuously worshipping God. They surround God's throne, constantly praising His holiness. Their chant, "Holy, holy, holy is the Lord Almighty," emphasizes God's purity and the intensity of His presence. This chant is a significant expression of the seraphim's deep reverence for God, highlighting His supreme sanctity.

I have two guardian seraphim angels, Soss and Otta, who were assigned to guide and protect me throughout my life on Earth and my spiritual journey afterward. Their role is to accompany me in this lifetime and as I transition through the mansion worlds toward ultimate spiritual enlightenment. Successfully guiding me on this journey to ascend allows them to ascend to higher roles and purposes as well.

I've seen souls and other divine manifestations by opening a portal and setting intentions during my meditations. My guardians, Soss and Otta, are responsible for orchestrating or staging, if you will, these experiences. They act as administrators, coordinating the content of what I see and interacting with other angels and entities to present these spiritual shows. This coordination is part of their duty to guide and enlighten me on my spiritual path.

I am often asked whether a person's religious background influences what they see or experience when interacting with something as abstract as a portal. I do believe that our personal beliefs and cultural backgrounds shape how we interpret and understand these experiences.

One of my mentors, Dr. Rebecca Martin, supports this notion by sharing her experiences. She explains that in her multiple lifetimes, her religious beliefs were always aligned with the religion she was born into in each life. For example, in her last life, she was born into a Catholic family, so her experiences and interpretations were influenced by Christian beliefs, including the figure of Jesus.

This suggests that our upbringing and the religious or cultural paradigms we grow up with significantly shape our consciousness. It affects how we perceive and interpret spiritual or mystical experiences, including what we might see in a portal.

Even for those who consider themselves anti-religious, the acknowledgement of figures such as Jesus indicates that religious concepts can influence anyone's perception, regardless of their current beliefs. This aligns with the broader idea that our cultural upbringing, religious beliefs, or ethnicity impacts how we interpret and understand experiences in our lives. The concept of portals for souls transitioning to a higher realm or state of being differs in the various religious and spiritual traditions beyond Christianity.

In Buddhism, ascension is closely tied to enlightenment and the cycle of rebirth. The ultimate goal is to achieve Nirvana, a state of liberation from the cycle of suffering and rebirth. While Buddhism does not explicitly describe physical portals, the journey to enlightenment can be seen as a spiritual pathway through which the soul ascends beyond the physical confines of existence.

Judaism offers a nuanced perspective on the afterlife, with interpretations varying among different Jewish traditions, ranging from the more mystical Kabbalistic views to the more historical and philosophical understandings of Rabbinic Judaism. While Judaism may not explicitly describe "portals" in the sense of physical gateways or doorways for the soul's ascent, the metaphorical pathways through ethical living, spiritual purification, and mystical journeying offer a rich conceptual framework for understanding how the soul progresses towards a closer communion with the Divine. In Jewish thought, the journey of the soul is intrinsically linked to the moral and spiritual development of the individual, the collective destiny of the Jewish people, and the ultimate redemption and perfection of the world.

Hinduism presents a rich tapestry of beliefs regarding the soul's journey after death, leading towards Moksha, liberation from the cycle of rebirth. The Garuda Purana, one of the texts that details afterlife beliefs, describes a complex cosmology with various realms and passages that the soul navigates through, guided by its karma. The concept of Yama, the God of death, and his realm can be seen as a portal through which souls transition, facing assessments before moving on to their next destination based on their actions in life.

In Taoism, the ascent of the soul is intricately linked with the pursuit of immortality and harmony with the Tao, the fundamental nature of the universe. The process involves spiritual cultivation and purification. The concept of Xian, or Taoist immortality, suggests a transformation or ascension of the soul to a higher state of being, which can be interpreted as passing through a spiritual portal toward a harmonious existence with the Tao.

Indigenous spiritualities often embrace the concept of a journey or transition of the soul to the spirit world. For instance, in many Native American traditions, the soul's journey after death includes moving through a specific landscape or path that leads to the spirit world, where ancestors and spiritual guides reside. These pathways are not just physical journeys but deeply spiritual ones, where the soul undergoes transformation and healing.

While these traditions vary widely in their beliefs and practices, the common thread is the understanding of death and the transition of the soul as a journey that involves moving through different states of being, often facilitated by spiritual guides, deities, or natural forces. These portals or pathways symbolize the soul's progression from the physical plane to a higher, more enlightened state.

Wanting to do my part and play a role in elevating the vibration of our world, I created a portal myself. It was a simple act of faith and intention. Every night I pray, focusing my thoughts on love, explicitly aiming to assist animals that have suffered or passed away. It is my hope that through this portal these souls can find their way to reunite with their families and friends in a peaceful, joyous place. And, of course, my desire to see Boo Boo again was a motivating factor for me initiating this practice.

In the beginning, the results of my efforts seemed unclear. I noticed only vague, dark shapes around the portal area for about a month, which I initially dismissed as mere shadows or blotches. However, as time passed, these shapes began to take on a more distinct form. My perception was adjusting, or perhaps the energy I channeled through the portal was manifesting in a way I could finally understand. These vague forms started to resemble animals reminiscent of cats or bears, creatures of the wild that now appeared to be navigating through the portal.

Moreover, I observed a brilliant light streaming down from the clouds above the portal. This light acted as a beacon, guiding the way for these spirit animals. Within this radiant glow, I could sometimes discern images, perhaps a bear or other guardian entities, which I realized were the portal's overseers or controllers. These beings, which I learned were known as midway creatures, played a crucial role in maintaining the balance and function of the portal, ensuring it served its purpose as a bridge for the animal souls moving on to their next existence.

This journey into creating and understanding the portal was not just an act of spiritual practice but a profound learning experience. It taught me about all life forms' interconnectedness, intention's power, and unseen forces that guide us toward compassion and higher understanding.

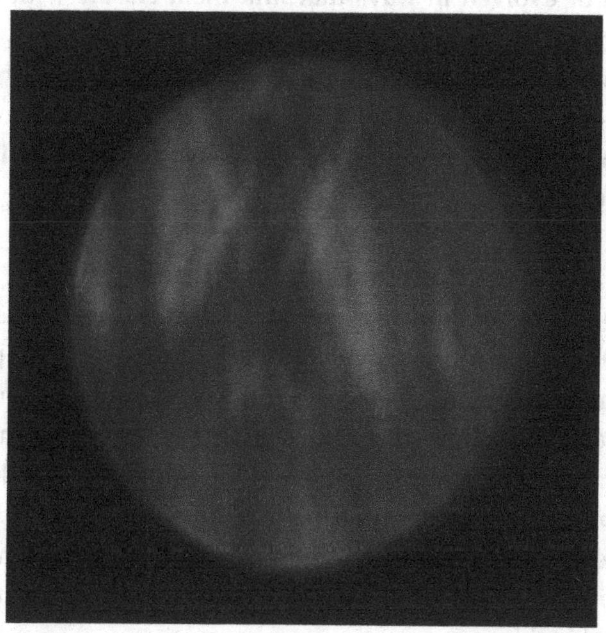

When I asked to see an angel, this is the first image I saw. Notice that the background looks like a church with people's hands in the air. This angel is above the altar. They showed me this so that I would understand that this is an angel in a holy place.

Midway Creatures

"Midwayers" occupy a unique position in the hierarchy of spiritual entities. They act as intermediaries between the mortal inhabitants of Earth and higher spiritual beings. Their role facilitates communication and interaction between the human world and the spiritual realm, making them an integral part of the spiritual ecosystem.

Nature and Origin

Midway creatures are so named because they exist midway between the material and spiritual worlds. They are considered to be of two types: primary and secondary. Primary midwayers are thought to have a direct origin in the spiritual realms, created or evolved in ways that link them closely with angels and other higher spiritual beings. Secondary midwayers, on the other hand, are believed to have more earthly origins. They are often described as being connected to the evolutionary progress of humanity itself, bridging the gap between the material and the ethereal.

Functions and Abilities

The functions of midway creatures are as diverse as their origins. They are often depicted as guardians of the planet, working silently and unseen to guide and protect humanity. Their abilities allow them to subtly influence the material world, nudging events, inspiring thoughts, and facilitating the work of higher spiritual beings. They are also said to be involved in the recording and preserving of human history, capturing the flow of events and human experiences for the spiritual archives.

Communication with Humans

One of the most intriguing aspects of midway creatures is their ability to communicate with humans. This communication is not direct but mediated through intuition, dreams, and sudden insights. People who are sensitive to spiritual energies or have developed their spiritual perception may become more aware of the presence and guidance of midway creatures. These interactions are often described as a sudden impulse to take a specific action, having a revelatory dream, or experiencing a profound sense of knowing without knowing why.

Role in Spiritual Development

Midway creatures are seen as allies and mentors in the spiritual development journey. They are believed to assist individuals in understanding more of the spiritual implications of their life experiences, helping them to navigate their personal growth and evolution. By acting as a bridge between the material and the spiritual, they help to make the abstract more tangible, providing insights that foster spiritual awakening and enlightenment.

Cultural and Philosophical Significance

The concept of midway creatures adds a rich layer to our understanding of the spiritual universe. It suggests that the cosmos is populated by a wide array of beings, each with a specific role in the cosmic order. The idea that entities are dedicated to assisting humanity in its spiritual evolution is comforting, offering a sense of connectedness and purpose in the vastness of existence.

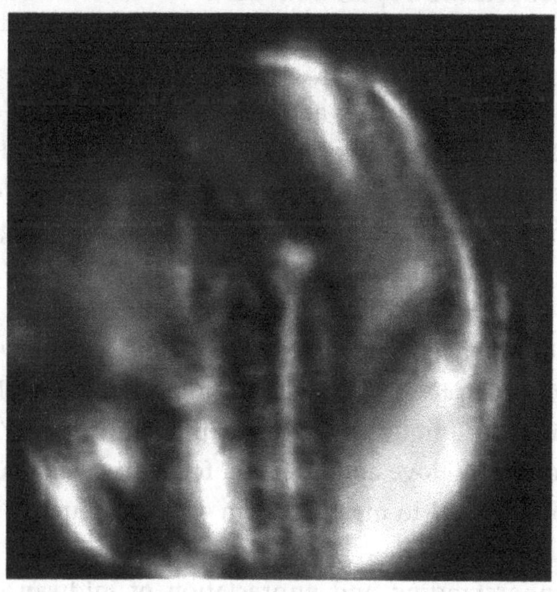

So many pictures have midway creatures in them. Do you see the woman in the upper right of this image?

What I Know to Be True of Midway Creatures

My perspective on midway creatures is deeply personal and stems from a profound experience. Initially, these beings were just abstract concepts to me, but they've become a vivid reality over time. When I first began to notice peculiar animals in various videos, particularly in contexts involving the movement of souls, I was intrigued yet puzzled. These creatures resembled familiar animals like wild cats, bears, and lions. Yet, they were distinctly different, with unique features such as spiked hair or tentacle-like appendages, reminiscent of *Star Wars* characters like Chewbacca.

My curiosity led me to the book *Urantia,* where I sought answers about these mysterious beings, which I later learned were midwayers. This journey of discovery revealed that they are not mere animals but significant entities in Earth's spiritual hierarchy, bridging mortals and angels. Their unique appearance sets them apart from Earth's wildlife, which I found fascinating and enlightening.

The roles of midwayers, especially during pivotal events like the rebellion of Lucifer and the narrative of Adam and Eve, intrigued me. Loyal midwayers retained their spiritual powers, serving as helpers and administrators under the guidance of seraphim. They collaborate with seraphim in soul guidance, although their presence might not be perceptible to humans during death or the transition to the afterlife.

They don't have names, at least not to me. They have always identified themselves with either numerical or alphabetical designations, a unique aspect of their identity that I've come to appreciate. My love and affection for midwayers has grown, and I look forward to meeting them after my journey on Earth ends.

My understanding and appreciation of midway creatures has evolved. I recognize them as integral and extraordinary participants in the spiritual realm, guiding souls and playing pivotal roles in the universe's grand narrative. In my reflections, I highlight the significance of both seraphim angels and midwayers, emphasizing their collaborative efforts in the cosmic framework.

Animals on the Other Side

Losing a dog is an experience that leaves an unfillable void in the heart of anyone who has had the privilege of sharing their life with such a faithful companion. A dog's heart and embodiment of unconditional love makes them become more than pets; they are family members, confidants, and sources of unbridled joy. The pain of their loss is intense, a testament to the depth of the bond formed over years of companionship.

When a dog passes away, he or she leaves behind a silence that echoes through the home, a presence sorely missed. Their absence is felt in every corner, from the spot on the couch where they napped to the sound of their paws on the floor. It's in the routine now broken, the walks not taken, the greetings not received. The void is not just physical but emotional.

The pain of losing a dog also reflects the selflessness they exude. They ask for little but give so much in return, teaching us about loyalty, resilience, and the importance of living in the moment. To lose such a teacher is to feel adrift, bereft of the simple, pure love that made the darkest days brighter and the good days even better.

This grief is a lonely journey, as the understanding of such a loss is not always recognized by those who have never experienced the unique companionship a dog provides. Yet, amid this deep sorrow, there's also a recognition of the gift of knowing such love. The pain of losing a dog is, in many ways, the cost of that love, a price willingly paid for the years of companionship, lessons learned, and unconditional love received. It's a reminder that to love deeply is to risk the pain of loss. Still, it's a risk that enriches our lives, teaching us about the depth of our capacity for love and the strength to endure its loss. The memory of a beloved dog becomes a treasure, a source of comfort and strength, as their spirit continues to guide and inspire long after they have gone.

In the quiet spaces of our hearts, where the pain of loss and the warmth of cherished memories reside, there exists a belief as comforting as it is mystical: that our departed dogs, now angels with invisible wings, find their way back to us through portals we create with our love and longing. These portals are not made of stone or wood but are woven from the threads of our deepest affections, unspoken wishes, and the silent prayers we send into the night sky.

Imagine, if you will, a world just beyond the reach of our senses, where our loyal companions run and play in fields of endless green, their spirits free of pain and filled with joy. This place, a paradise reserved for the purest of souls, is connected to our world by the love that never fades, even in the face of loss. When our longing aligns with the magic of the universe, and our intention is that of love and only love, we can create a portal through which our dog angels can visit us.

At other times, these visits are subtle, often felt rather than seen, a gentle nudge in the stillness of the night, a soft rustling in the air, or the faintest sound of paws padding alongside us. Some find solace in a dream where a beloved face appears, eyes shining with love, and a tail wagging in joy, a message that all is well on the other side. Others might feel a warm presence, an inexplicable comfort during moments of sorrow as if a soft, furry head rests again against their leg.

Creating these portals requires no special rituals, only an open heart and a willingness to believe in the unseen. In our moments of deepest reflection, when the veil between worlds seems thinnest, we might sense their presence most strongly. By holding onto the love we shared, cherishing the memories, and letting the tears flow when they come, we keep the portal open, a beacon of love that shines across dimensions.

These dog angels, guardians of our hearts, remind us that love transcends physical boundaries and that our connections to those we have lost are not severed by death but transformed. They teach us that what many people have quoted is true: "Grief and love are two sides of the same coin." And that currency buys us moments of ethereal reunion, glimpses of a love that never dies.

In this way, our beloved dogs continue to guide us, not just through past memories but as angels who watch over us, their love a bridge between worlds. And in the quiet moments when we feel their presence, we are reminded that we are never truly apart.

In *The Amazing Afterlife of Animals,* Karen A. Anderson writes, "The other side is where our animal's energy exists after their physical body dies. It is another dimension – also referred to as Heaven or Eternity – that overlaps our atmosphere. Once an animal leaves its body, there are many entry and exit points, called portals, through which their energy, or soul, travels between Earth and the other side. The animals tell me they can appear just about anywhere here on Earth. They can move back and forth between our dimension and theirs with ease. For example, they can choose their favorite bed, chair, or windowsill. Some like to re-enter outside portals in the yard, such as a field, the barn, or any other place where they spent a lot of time."

The portal I have created acts as a bridge for animals during their transitional moments. Looking at my portal, I've seen thousands of animals. I see my beloved Boo Boo all the time. Sometimes, I'll see a bear with a lion in the clouds, acting as protectors of this sacred space. These spirit guardians watch over the gateway, making me curious about their roles and attention towards me.

I realized they're showing thanks for the gateway I've made, helping them move toward their next phase. Understanding this, I've encouraged them towards their journey ahead. As I have stated earlier, this gateway isn't just a path; it represents our shared growth, moving towards a higher state of awareness and kindness. Our compassion leads the way as the Earth shifts towards this new phase. Happily, I have felt a change in the world's energy lately. It has become lighter and more liberated. This reflects the enduring spirit's ability to overcome challenges. Guided by our inner light, this journey unfolds, showing the endless possibilities of a world in tune with its spirit.

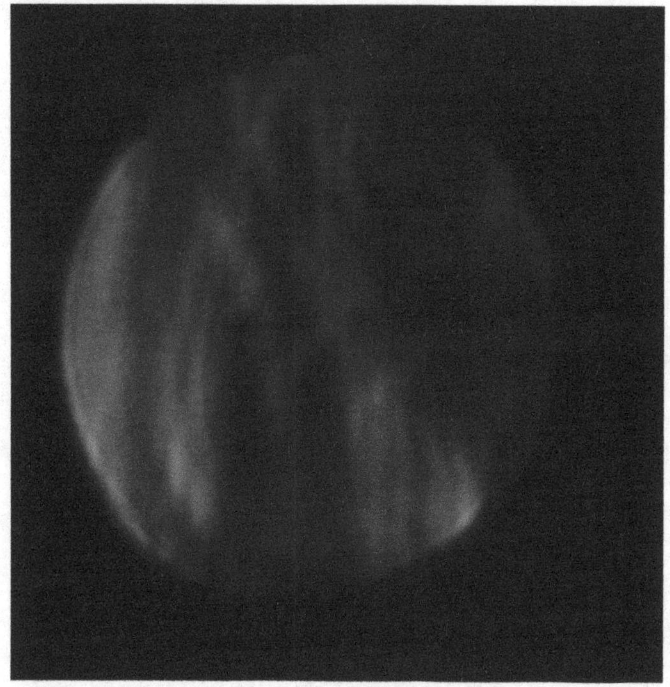

The Lion's Gate – one of my favorites. On 8/8 the Lion's Gate opens up. This occurs when Sirius, Earth, and the sun in the sign of Leo align with the great Pyramids of Giza and the Sphinx. I meditated and asked to see this phenomenon and the Holy Ones projected this. Three lions' heads are seen in the upper right and the largest one is sending energy down to a kneeling girl with long hair.

The genesis of this entire journey can be traced back to my love for Boo Boo. It's a testament to the power of love and emotion, which, as seen through the lens of the divine matrix, serves as the fundamental connection between us all. This truly astonishing concept underscores the emotion-driven nature of our existence and interactions.

Boo Boo in the mist

The Divine Matrix Explained

Gregg Braden is an American author known for his work bridging science, spirituality, and the real world. In his book, *The Divine Matrix,* he merges the insights of ancient wisdom with the discoveries of modern science to present a compelling view of the universe. He suggests that the universe is an interconnected network, not merely a collection of isolated parts. This network vibrates with energy, linking everything from individual thoughts to the cosmos.

Central to Braden's thesis is the concept that our beliefs directly influence our reality. He proposes that how we think and feel shapes our perception of the world and the world itself. This idea empowers us to change our reality by adopting positive beliefs, suggesting that our perspective on life can actively shape our experiences.

The Divine Matrix refers to the energy field that connects all things. Braden compares this field to a cosmic Internet, through which our thoughts, actions, and emotions transmit signals across space and time, impacting the universe in profound ways. This concept implies that we are far more interconnected with the fabric of reality than we might have previously thought.

Quantum physics supports these notions by illustrating a universe filled with endless possibilities that only become reality when observed. Braden argues that by focusing on our intentions, we can choose from these possibilities and actively participate in creating our reality. This shifts us from passive observers to active creators, working with the universe to manifest our desires.

Emotions play a crucial role in this process, acting as a language through which we communicate with the universe. Braden suggests positive emotions can heal and harmonize, while negative emotions can cause imbalance and discord. This elevates emotions from simple reactions to powerful tools for change, capable of affecting our well-being and the world.

Braden also shares stories of miraculous events attributed to the power of belief and intention, illustrating the untapped potential within us to bring about significant changes in our reality. These anecdotes reinforce his message that belief can lead to real-world miracles, aligning our reality with our highest aspirations.

A key message in Braden's work is the idea of a global consciousness, an emerging awareness of our interconnectedness that could lead to profound global change. He encourages us to embrace our role as co-creators of our world, envisioning a future of harmony and peace.

Through *The Divine Matrix*, Gregg Braden invites us to view the world anew, emphasizing the power of thought, belief, and emotion to shape our reality. He presents a pathway to a more harmonious existence, highlighting our potential to influence the broader framework of life significantly.

Creating Your Own Portal

The first step is to ensure that you have a clear purpose that benefits everyone involved. This purpose should be rooted in love and aimed at the highest good for the individual, their family, and others.

Once the purpose is defined, the portal should facilitate the flow between our world and the spirit world. This could involve sending love and intentions to loved ones who have passed away, or asking for positive energies like love and joy to be brought into one's life through the portal.

The key to creating a portal is focus. Think of it as a funnel that gathers and directs these energies. This means concentrating on your intentions and desires, ensuring they align with the principles of love and the greater good, and envisioning them moving through the portal to achieve the desired outcome.

Portals, according to Diana Cooper, can be created intentionally through meditation, visualization, and the invocation of angels, archangels, and ascended masters. Individuals can establish sacred spaces that amplify spiritual energies and facilitate deeper connections with the divine by connecting with these higher beings and focusing on love, light, and healing. These portals can be used for various purposes, such as enhancing personal healing, accelerating spiritual development, and sending healing energies to the Earth.

Cooper emphasizes the importance of purity of intention and the alignment with divine will when creating and working with portals. The energy and consciousness level of the individual play a crucial role in the portal's effectiveness and vibrational quality. By raising one's vibration through meditation, affirmations, and acts of kindness, one can ensure that the portals created are of the highest light and serve the highest good.

Furthermore, Cooper suggests that these portals also enable the receipt of higher wisdom and divine messages, thus assisting individuals on their spiritual journey by providing guidance and clarity. The creation of portals is not just for the individual's benefit. Still, it is also seen as a service to the planet, helping to anchor light and love on Earth and supporting its transition into the "New Golden Age."

Creating a portal is not a prerequisite for connecting with entities from the spiritual realm. However, a specific timeframe is considered more conducive for such communications: between 3 to 4 a.m. This period is often recommended for those seeking to interact with a loved one who has passed, encounter an angel, receive guidance, experience a vision, or embark on an out-of-body journey.

The rationale behind this timing lies in the state of our minds during these early morning hours. Unlike the initial phase of sleep when our minds are bustling with the day's thoughts and concerns, the period from 3 to 4 a.m. brings a different level of quietude. In the early parts of the night, our thoughts can be scattered and restless, reflecting the chaos of our daily lives. As the night progresses, we enter deeper phases of sleep, where the conscious mind quiets down, allowing for a unique state of stillness and receptivity.

This tranquility is why the predawn hours are ideal for spiritual communication. In this state of deep sleep, transitioning into a slight wakefulness while retaining the calm and stillness of the mind creates an optimal condition for connecting with spiritual guides, angels, or loved ones who have passed on. During this time, the veil between the physical and spiritual worlds is perceived to be thinner, facilitating clearer communication and more profound spiritual experiences.

For those looking to engage with their guardian angels or spirit guides, waking up during this window and consciously setting the intention to communicate can be particularly powerful. The quiet of these hours, free from the distractions and the noise of the day, allows for a more focused and sincere connection with the spiritual realm. Whether seeking advice, comfort, or a deeper spiritual experience, this time offers a unique opportunity for those willing to explore their spirituality in the quiet of the night.

As we draw this chapter to a close, we delve into the profound realization that the journey beyond the physical realm is not an end but a transition through gateways and portals that lead us into a new world unseen by the naked eye. These gateways are not mere figments of our imagination but pivotal bridges that allow for exchanging messages and wisdom from those who have already crossed over to the other side. They serve as a medium for us to commune with our spirit guides and angels, entities that guide us with an unseen hand and provide comfort and counsel in times of need.

The existence of these portals came to life for me in a deeply personal way through my experiences with Boo Boo. The grief that once enveloped my heart, leaving a void that seemed impossible to fill, began to heal through the uplifting and serene encounters facilitated by these gateways. It was in these moments of spiritual connection that I felt Boo Boo's presence beside me, not as a memory of the past but as a vibrant spirit accompanying me in the now. The knowledge that she is always with me, transcending the physical world's limitations, has been a source of immense comfort and healing.

This journey from grief to healing underscores a universal truth about love and loss. It reveals that the bonds we form are eternal, stretching beyond the confines of physical existence. The ability to receive messages and visit with our spirit guides and angels through these portals illuminates a path of personal healing and transformation. It offers a glimpse into the continuity of life and love, affirming that those we hold dear remain intertwined with our souls, guiding and watching over us.

In embracing the existence of these gateways, we open ourselves to a world of spiritual enlightenment and connection. We learn that every goodbye is not the end but a transition to a different form of presence in our lives. The journey of healing from the loss of Boo Boo has taught me that love is the bridge that connects us to the other side, a bridge that is always there, waiting to be crossed whenever we seek the comfort and guidance of those who have gone before us. Therefore, this chapter is not just a conclusion but an invitation to view the other side, not as a distant realm but as a space of continuous love, guidance, and reunion, forever changing our perception of loss and the afterlife.

Chapter 7

What Happens When You Die?

Energy cannot be created or destroyed; it can only be changed from one form to another.

Albert Einstein

I have never had a near-death experience (NDE) myself, but I'm really interested in what happens after we die. This has led me to read a lot about other people's NDEs. These stories from people who've come close to dying often talk about incredible experiences and give us some clues about what might happen when we pass away.

In this chapter, we'll examine what some of these people have reported seeing and feeling during their NDEs to get a better idea of what the afterlife might be like. We'll also examine common experiences like life reviews, meeting other beings, and the sense of peace many describe. While I haven't experienced these things myself, the detailed accounts from those who have can provide valuable insights.

By examining these stories, I aim to piece together what the journey after death might entail, recognizing that I still don't know. Even though I'm still very much alive, learning about these experiences makes me think that death could be just another phase in our existence, leading us into a new, unexplored chapter of our journey.

Your Brain While Dying

In a groundbreaking study that has captured the attention of neuroscientists worldwide, a team led by Dr. Raul Vicente at the University of Tartu (Estonia) and Dr. Ajmal Zemmar at the University of Louisville has achieved a significant milestone by recording the brain activity of a human as they passed away. This unprecedented observation was made in Vancouver, Canada, during the monitoring of an 87-year-old epilepsy patient who, following an accidental fall, suffered a fatal heart attack while under continuous electroencephalography (EEG) surveillance.

This research has unveiled fascinating insights into the brain's behavior during the final moments of life, suggesting a phenomenon much like the commonly described "life flashing before one's eyes." In the crucial period surrounding the cessation of the heart's function, researchers observed a surge in brain activity, notably in gamma oscillations, a type of brainwave associated with memory recall, alongside other brainwave patterns like delta, theta, alpha, and beta oscillations. These findings hint at a possible intrinsic capacity of the brain to orchestrate a final cognitive recollection or "life recall," potentially offering a scientific basis for experiences reported during near-death situations.

The implications of this study extend beyond the neuroscientific, touching on ethical considerations in medical practice, such as determining the moment of death in contexts like organ donation protocols.

Dr. Zemmar's work, detailed in the study "Enhanced Interplay of Neuronal Coherence and Coupling in the Dying Human Brain," published in *Frontiers in Aging Neuroscience,* opens new avenues for understanding the intersection of cognitive function, consciousness, and the cessation of life. It raises profound questions about the timing of death, the potential continuity of brain activity post-cardiac arrest, and the implications for defining death legally and medically.

This research adds a significant chapter to our understanding of death. It offers comfort, suggesting a possible cognitive serenity in the final moments. It reassures those facing the loss of loved ones that their final experiences could be filled with meaningful recollections. This discovery, therefore, not only advances our scientific knowledge but also touches on our existence's spiritual and philosophical dimensions, offering a new perspective on the universal experience of death.

Near-Death Experiences

The phenomenon of near-death experiences has intrigued the scientific community, leading to a spectrum of theories attempting to explain their occurrence. On one end, some scientists argue that NDEs are physiological, triggered by the brain's response to extreme stress or trauma. They suggest that specific neurochemical processes or the brain's end-of-life activity might create the vivid and often intense experiences reported during NDEs.

On the other hand, psychologically, researchers propose that NDEs could be a form of coping mechanism, offering comfort during moments of intense danger or stress. Some theories delve into the transcendental realm, suggesting that NDEs might glimpse another layer of reality or existence, pointing towards the possibility of life after death or the survival of consciousness beyond the physical body.

Individuals who have experienced near-death experiences often recount transformative encounters marked by vivid realism and profound emotional and spiritual revelations. They frequently report sensations of peace, encounters with luminous entities or divine presences usually identified as God or Jesus, and life reviews that reflect their earthly actions and ripple effects. Contrary to a hazy or undefined afterlife, these experiences are described as exceptionally clear and real, suffused with an intense sense of love and an acute clarity of memory.

While there are commonalities in these accounts, such as traveling through a tunnel or floating above one's body, each narrative maintains its unique personal details, from meeting deceased relatives to receiving guidance from otherworldly beings. These experiences challenge conventional views of existence, suggesting a continuity of consciousness that transcends our physical boundaries.

About 23% of people reporting NDEs describe entering one of several distinct realms, hinting at an afterlife structured in stages of learning and progression rather than a simple heaven-hell dichotomy. These realms are depicted as places of unmatched beauty and serenity, where souls undergo growth and enlightenment, potentially over numerous lifetimes, deepening their understanding of the universe.

This intricate view of the afterlife posits that our earthly actions and the lessons we accrue across lifetimes shape our journey beyond death. The experiences recounted in NDEs offer a look into what might lie beyond death and provide a profound opportunity for introspection and understanding, enriching our grasp of human consciousness and the interconnected fabric of existence. Many who experience NDEs report profound life changes afterward. They may have a different outlook on life, a decreased fear of death, and an increased sense of purpose or spirituality.

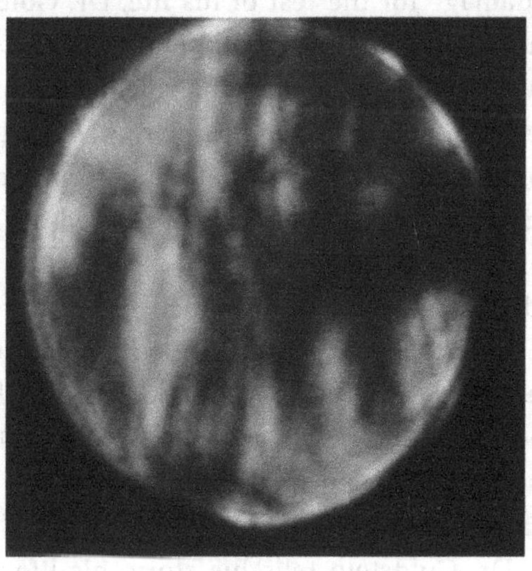

From left to right you see Archangel Ariel and four midway creatures.

Dr. Marcy Goldstein

One illustrative story is about a renowned plastic surgeon from St. Louis. Dr. Marcy Goldstein was in a traumatic car accident in which he had to be pried out of the car by the "Jaws of Life." He was found unresponsive, and he had broken every bone in his body except one arm, one leg, and his spine.

In the ensuing days, spinal fluid started leaking from his ears and the doctors reported that he suffered severe brain damage. He fell in and out of a coma while in the intensive care unit for 3½ months, and it was during that time that he had his near-death experience, he later told friends.

He painted a picture of being wholly enveloped with the warmest, most loving white light, and he described the most wonderful feeling in his chest that he never felt again. He couldn't wait to go back and he spent the rest of his life telling anyone who would listen that there is more to our journey than our present physical bodies.

It took two long years, but despite being told by the doctors that he would never walk properly again, and that he would have brain damage for the rest of his life, Dr. Goldstein made a miraculous 100% recovery, both mentally and physically. Although Western medicine played a role, he gave most of the credit to the acupuncture treatments he received. Most notably, traveling to England to receive treatments from world-famous acupuncturist, Dr. J.R. Worsley. He considered his recovery an unmistakable miracle.

Dr. Goldstein returned to his practice, but after a year he realized he was no longer being fulfilled as a plastic surgeon. He had started incorporating acupuncture into his practice before the accident, and now wanted to devote his time to only practice Eastern medicine from then on, for it was what brought him the greatest joy.

The way Dr. Goldstein tells his story, his life was forever changed. His decision was an easy one to understand really:

He wanted to spend the rest of his life feeling the same joy he experienced during that NDE, and healing his patients through acupuncture did just that.

Dr. Goldstein's experience changed his consciousness completely. He had a new understanding that life should be lived to the fullest, and he didn't want to waste a second longer doing something that no longer made him happy. This decision led him to become one of the most widely respected acupuncturists. His story and other out-of-body experiences highlight the impactful and transformative nature of these encounters.

Lessons from the Light

I absolutely loved *Lessons from the Light: What We Can Learn from the Near-Death Experience* by Kenneth Ring and Evelyn Elsaesser Valarino. It is a comprehensive exploration of near-death experiences and their profound impact on individuals' lives. The book delves into various aspects of NDEs, providing insights into what people commonly report and how these experiences transform them.

Key takeaways from the book include:

1. **Common Elements of NDEs:** The book outlines typical features of NDEs, such as the sensation of leaving the body, moving through a tunnel, encountering a brilliant light, communicating with deceased loved ones or spiritual beings, and experiencing a life review.
2. **Transformational Effects:** Individuals who undergo NDEs often experience significant changes in their values, attitudes, and perceptions of life and death afterwards. The book discusses how these experiences lead to a greater appreciation for life, a diminished fear of death, and an enhanced sense of purpose.
3. **Universality and Diversity:** The book highlights that while NDEs have common core elements, they also vary

across cultures and individuals, reflecting a diversity of backgrounds and beliefs.

4. **Aftereffects:** NDE experiencers frequently report long-lasting positive and challenging aftereffects. Positive changes include increased spirituality, compassion, and a sense of interconnectedness. Some face difficulties in readjusting to everyday life due to the profound nature of their experiences.
5. **The Light:** The encounter with a light or being of light is often described as an encounter with unconditional love and profound wisdom. The book explores the significance of this encounter in the context of personal transformation and spiritual insight.
6. **Scientific and Spiritual Perspectives:** The authors discuss NDEs from both scientific and spiritual viewpoints, acknowledging the ongoing debate about their nature – whether they are neurological phenomena, transcendental experiences, or a combination of both.
7. **Implications for Living:** The book emphasizes the lessons that NDEs offer to those who have not experienced them, suggesting that the insights gained from these experiences can improve one's approach to life, relationships, and personal growth.

Lessons from the Light serves as a resource for understanding the profound impact of NDEs and offers readers a deeper appreciation of the lessons these experiences provide, encouraging a more compassionate, meaningful, and mindful approach to life.

When We Die

At the point of death, we leave behind our physical bodies and earthly egos, shedding our earthly existence's accumulated beliefs and paradigms. This transition marks a release from the material world, moving into a new realm where care and nurturing continue, albeit in a different form. When you die, your memories remain intact. Still, you shed your physical or "heavy" body and transition into a "light" body.

According to the book *Urantia,* when we die, we embark on a new phase of existence that extends far beyond our time on Earth. This journey isn't just a continuation but an adventure filled with learning and progression, as described below:

The Journey Begins

The journey after death is meticulously orchestrated, involving specific energies and guided by celestial beings like seraphim, angels, and potentially other spiritual entities. This guided transition through a tunnel signifies the soul's passage to the afterlife, shaped by one's earthly actions and karma, which influence the nature of this experience. Noteworthy spiritual figures, such as Jesus or God, may guide souls during this transition, providing direction for what comes next.

In the afterlife, the soul enters what are known as the mansion worlds, realms that serve as platforms for continued learning and growth rather than mere waypoints. These worlds function not unlike schools for the soul, offering lessons on spiritual evolution and cosmic understanding far beyond what earthly experiences can teach. Here, the focus is on the soul's development and progression through these unique stages of the afterlife, each designed to facilitate deeper comprehension and growth.

The Mansion Worlds

"In my Father's house are many mansions: if it were not so, I would have told you. I go to prepare a place for you. And if I go and prepare a place for you, I will come again and receive you unto myself; where I am, there ye may be also." This passage from the New Testament of the Bible, specifically from the

Gospel of John, chapter 14, verses 2–3, is often interpreted as Jesus comforting his disciples, promising them a place in heaven after his departure. The phrase "my Father's house" symbolizes heaven, and the "many mansions" suggest the idea of different levels or stages of spiritual existence.

Each of the seven distinct "mansion worlds" serves as a stage for our continued growth and learning. These realms can be likened to different levels in a video game, where advancement is based on the acquisition of knowledge, understanding, and spiritual insights rather than the accumulation of points or the completion of tasks.

Each mansion world presents its own lessons and experiences specifically tailored to aid the soul's development. As we navigate through these worlds, we encounter various challenges and opportunities designed to foster our growth, much like a student progresses through grades in school, mastering one level before moving on to the next.

In these realms, we're not passive participants but active learners, engaging with the environment, its inhabitants, and the lessons each world offers. The journey is individual and collective as we interact with other souls, sharing experiences and learning from one another.

This progression isn't just about personal advancement; it's also about understanding the interconnectedness of all things and deepening our comprehension of the universe's vast mysteries. As we move from one mansion world to the next, we shed old limitations and expand our consciousness, preparing for whatever lies ahead in this grand cosmic journey.

The concept of mansion worlds provides a framework for envisioning the afterlife as a dynamic and purposeful continuation of our existence, where growth, learning, and evolution are central themes. This perspective offers comfort and motivation, suggesting that our journey doesn't end with physical death but transitions into a new, enriching phase of exploration and discovery.

Transitioning from Physical to Morontia

Morontia is a term from *Urantia* that refers to a state between the physical and the spiritual. As you progress through the mansion worlds, you evolve from a physical being to a morontia being — this is a vital part of your journey towards becoming an entirely spiritual entity. Once you've passed, you will encounter one or more individuals who will assist you in reviewing your life. This review isn't just a recap; it's an in-depth analysis of every moment, both good and bad, and a reflection on your actions, achievements, and areas where you could have improved. This process is integral to your spiritual progression, helping you advance through the mansion worlds toward achieving spiritual perfection and ultimately reaching the paradise world.

These experiences are particularly profound and rewarding for those who have lived with love and purpose, acting as "lightworkers" during their earthly lives. The individuals you meet in this phase could be members of your soul family, providing support and insight as you assess your life's journey.

After the review, your next destination in the afterlife is determined. This transition often involves passing through a tunnel of light, a common element in near-death experiences that many find comforting and familiar.

First Steps in the Afterlife

Once through the tunnel, if you're not experiencing a near-death moment but have indeed passed on, you're greeted by familiar faces. These beings, including family members, friends, and pets who have passed before you, welcome you. Interestingly, they often appear in their prime, choosing to present themselves as they were during their best years, not necessarily as they were at the time of their passing.

The environment of this reunion is comforting and familiar, tailored to your personal memories and comfort zones. And while the setting may vary from person to person, the essence of warmth and welcome remains constant.

It's said that angels begin notifying your loved ones in the afterlife to prepare for your arrival before your passing. This advance notice helps them gather and be ready to greet you when you cross over.

Upon arrival, there's a period where you can explore, meet with loved ones who have passed before you, and get ready for what's next. It's like orientation day at a new school. Then, you dive into the actual learning and growing process.

The Ultimate Goal

This journey aims to attain a state of perfection and discover the divine presence in Paradise, the ultimate destination. Along this route, you'll encounter chances for rest, healing, and ongoing education, all intended to ready you for further elevation in the universe's vast plan. This continuous voyage focuses not only on personal enlightenment but also on contributing to the broader cosmic community.

Learning in the afterlife isn't trivial; it encompasses deep insights into the universe, the creation of planets, and other cosmic truths, all contributing to a soul's journey toward spiritual purity. Despite this profound journey, individuals retain their memories and aspects of their identity, which helps maintain a sense of continuity.

When a soul reaches the seventh mansion world, it has undergone a significant transformation, adopting a new form while retaining core aspects of its previous existence. Even as a "new" soul, one's memories and personal traits persist, aiding the progression through these realms.

Interaction isn't limited to familiar faces; souls can engage with beings from other planets, enhancing their learning and understanding of the universe. These encounters are part of the soul's educational journey, enriching their experience and knowledge as they move through different levels of existence.

A Universal Family

The concept of the afterlife, particularly the idea of mansion worlds, introduces a profoundly comforting notion that in the post-mortem phase, all individuals, irrespective of their diverse paths and experiences on Earth, converge into a harmonious, unified collective. This convergence isn't merely a gathering; it's a shared journey of enlightenment where every soul, connected in a newfound celestial kinship, engages in an ongoing learning and mutual growth process.

This perspective on the afterlife reframes the end of our physical lives as a mere transition, marking the beginning of a new, enriching chapter focused on continual personal and spiritual development. It's a vision that imbues the afterlife with purpose and progression, offering solace in the idea that our existence extends beyond the physical realm into a more significant and collective experience of growth.

This elaborate afterlife blueprint, with its emphasis on structured growth, unity, and progression toward a divine culmination, offers a profound and optimistic outlook on existence. It suggests that every moment, every experience, and every lesson is a step on an eternal journey of learning, development, and spiritual ascendance.

Heaven and Hell

The teachings about heaven and hell in *Urantia* have greatly impacted my understanding of life and what might follow it. *Urantia*'s depiction moves beyond traditional ideas of heaven and hell, which often focus on reward and punishment, to present an afterlife centered on personal development, enlightenment, and the soul's progression. This resonates with my core belief in a universe that is inherently fair, filled with love, and dedicated to the continuous advancement of every creature within it.

In *Urantia,* heaven is not simply a destination where one enjoys eternal bliss; it's portrayed as a dynamic process of ongoing spiritual evolution across diverse realms. This idea inspires me, suggesting that our journey extends into a vast expanse of learning opportunities and transformative experiences. It imbues my daily life with meaning and direction, reinforcing that our earthly decisions and deeds echo into our post-mortem existence.

Moreover, *Urantia*'s interpretation of hell as a state of spiritual inertia or a conscious detachment from divine love, rather than a place of endless suffering, prompts me to live consciously, valuing compassion and integrity. It highlights the necessity of living harmoniously with our core principles and contributing constructively to our environment and people.

These insights motivate me to perceive my existence, and that of others, with greater compassion and understanding, appreciating our diverse spiritual journeys. The afterlife, as depicted in *Urantia,* encourages me to embrace each day with curiosity and a zeal for self-improvement, fully aware that our soul's voyage is far more expansive and intricate than our earthly experiences might suggest. This perspective enriches my present life and offers a comforting and optimistic outlook on the eternal journey that awaits us all.

Animals in the Afterlife

My investigations into the afterlife experiences of animals have unveiled a captivating journey orchestrated by seraphim angels. One night I was shown an amazing image of two animals bathed in a radiant, welcoming light, reinforcing my understanding that animals, including my cherished Boo Boo, traverse a path of light upon their departure from our world, similar to human experiences. This pathway also leads them to an exclusive animal realm, a mansion world where they find comfort and camaraderie.

In this distinct afterlife dimension, animals are reunited with familiar faces from their past, echoing the human experience of post-mortem reunions. However, a remarkable aspect of their afterlife existence is their ability to concurrently inhabit dual realms. This duality implies that while I look forward to reuniting with Boo Boo, she is also delighting in the companionship of other animals in a separate, blissful dimension. This ability of animals to engage in various realms simultaneously suggests a complex and shared journey of the soul, extending beyond human experiences to encompass all sentient beings.

The notion that my connection with Boo Boo will endure beyond physical death is a source of deep comfort to me. Anticipating a reunion in an afterlife free from earthly encumbrances, where joy and love prevail, affirms the enduring nature of our bond, untouched by physical parting. The afterlife, as I've come to understand it, is a space where learning, growth, and evolution are central themes experienced by humans and animals alike. This process of continual soul progression hints at a broader, universal journey of enlightenment and transformation.

The resemblance in behavior and personality between my new dog and Boo Boo reinforces my belief in the continuation of Boo Boo's soul essence. Anticipating a future encounter with her distinct spirit in the afterlife highlights our existence's layered and multidimensional reality, extending far beyond our immediate, tangible world. This perspective not only comforts but also celebrates the ongoing connections we share with our animal companions, underscoring a bond that surpasses the confines of the physical world and weaves into the expansive, interconnected fabric of the afterlife.

Choices

I touched upon this fascinating idea earlier in the chapter: A day or two before you pass away, your soul departs from your body to inform your loved ones on the other side that you'll soon be joining them. It's like sending a heads-up to everyone in the spiritual realm to gather around and prepare to welcome you as you pass through the tunnel to the other side.

When discussing what happens after death, particularly regarding angels, there's much to consider about souls' choices. Commonly, people can head towards the light immediately after they pass or stay around for a bit. It's not rare for souls to remain present to observe their own funerals or visit loved ones before moving on to the light.

Some individuals go directly to the light, while others might linger on Earth. This lingering can occur for various reasons. For instance, if someone dies suddenly in a traumatic event, like a car accident, they might not realize they've passed away. There are stories of spirits or ghosts seen in places tied to sudden or violent deaths.

Historical sites, like the Vanderbilt family's mansion in Rhode Island, are known for such occurrences. Despite being a place of beauty, it has a history of tragic deaths, and visitors, including my wife, have experienced unexplained cold spots, believed to be the spirits of family members who remain attached to the location.

Another example is a lady who adored her home and seemed to continue residing there after her death, as evidenced by unusual occurrences and her distinctive image captured in a photograph during Christmas, a time laden with happy memories for her.

In essence, after death, individuals have choices: they can move towards the light, stay to observe or interact with the living for a time, or, in some cases, remain attached to specific places or memories. While the presence of angels and spiritual guidance is a comforting notion for many, each soul's journey is unique and influenced by their life experiences and decisions.

In *Lessons from the Light,* there's a notable account from author Norman Paulsen. He describes a life-altering experience where he encountered a massive, radiant sphere. He heard a voice asking if he was ready to die and be with the divine presence. He responded affirmatively, feeling no fear and ready to embrace what he loved most. This sphere of light enveloped him in brightness, far surpassing anything he had ever witnessed, drawing him into its luminosity. This account supports the idea that orbs play a significant role in the afterlife, as vehicles transporting souls.

Connecting to a Loved One

Suppose you're interested in having an out-of-body experience to reconnect with a loved one who has passed, like a grandparent. In that case, there's a process you might try. For instance, I wanted to see my grandmother. When she appeared to me during these experiences, she chose to show herself as a young and vibrant woman. That was expected because, as noted earlier, spirits often prefer to present themselves in their prime. To initiate this kind of experience, visualize climbing a ladder and pushing yourself out towards the ceiling. This visualization can help facilitate an out-of-body experience where you can encounter your loved ones.

Interestingly, when these loved ones appear, they may choose environments or activities that reflect their younger years. For example, I saw my father on a golf course, appearing younger and engaging in an activity he enjoyed. This shows that spirits can interact with us in scenarios that are meaningful to them and us.

To enhance your chances of success, set your intention before going to sleep, specifically asking to meet with your loved one. While it might not happen immediately, persistence is key. The spiritual realm operates under its own laws, and your ability to connect can be influenced by your own spiritual progress and the nature of your intentions.

Dreams versus Visions

Based on my personal experiences, I've observed a few notable differences in distinguishing between dreams and visions. Visions typically occur in the early morning hours, often between 2 and 3 a.m. This timing seems significant in differentiating them from the usual dream cycle.

Dreams often appear murky or unclear, with a fog-like quality that makes them hard to recall in detail. In contrast, visions are remarkably clear and vivid. They feature bright, distinct colors and sharp details, creating a memorable and impactful experience. The clarity of visions extends beyond the moment of waking; you remember these visions in striking detail immediately upon waking and well into the following day. This lasting impression is one of the key characteristics that help distinguish a vision from ordinary dreams.

Deathbed Visions

In the March 17th, 2024 issue of *The New York Times Magazine,* journalist Phoebe Zerwick highlights a profound experience some individuals can experience at the end of their lives, and when witnessed, are described as deathbed visions. These experiences, often dismissed by medical professionals as delusions or hallucinations, are revealed through the personal and research narratives of Chris Kerr, a medical doctor who has studied these phenomena extensively.

The article starts with Kerr's personal encounter with a deathbed vision when he was a child at his dying father's bedside. Kerr grew up in Toronto with a father who was a busy surgeon and had limited time to spend with him, except for their cherished annual fishing trips to the Canadian wilderness. When his father was 42 and weakened by cancer, he spoke of preparing for another trip to their cabin as he fiddled with Kerr's shirt buttons. This occurred during a poignant moment in the hospital, where a priest intervened, suggesting his father was delusional. Kerr's father passed away the next morning. Reflecting back, Kerr believes this was not delusion but an end-of-life vision, signaling a meaningful, if not spiritual, connection to their shared experiences.

This early experience laid the foundation for his later research in this field, where he observed similar visions among patients at Hospice & Palliative Care Buffalo. Kerr's research indicates that such visions are quite common, with a significant percentage of hospice patients reporting experiences that provide them comfort, meaning, and sometimes reconciliation with past events.

Kerr's studies, documented through interviews and observations, suggest that these visions are distinct from hallucinations caused by medication or neurological issues. They often involve encounters with deceased loved ones or revisitations of significant life events, bringing peace and a sense of closure to the dying. Importantly, Kerr's work challenges the medical community's skepticism, highlighting a need to acknowledge and respect these experiences as part of the dying process. This offers insights not only into death but into the essence of living.

These narratives underscore the emotional and spiritual growth experienced by individuals with these visions, suggesting a paradox where physical decline at life's end is accompanied by psychological and spiritual expansion. Kerr's observations offer a compelling case for the importance of these visions in providing comfort, affirming life's meaning, and facilitating a dignified transition at the end of life.

How Do You Interpret the Images You See?

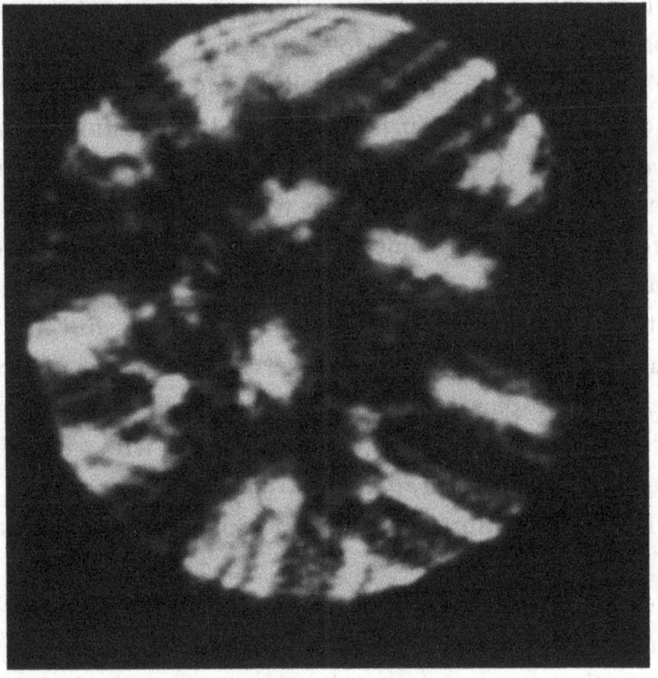

When I was reading Gregg Braden's book, *The Divine Matrix*, my Holy Ones showed me this pattern that mimics the flower of life.

Here's a breakdown of what you might be seeing and questioning:

1. **What are we seeing?** Suppose you're referring to images or phenomena captured in videos or described in books. In that case, you might see representations or interpretations of various afterlife realms. These could be artistic or visionary depictions of a soul's stages after death.
2. **Images from one of the realms?** The images could be conceptual representations of one or more of these realms. Since each level offers different experiences and

lessons for the soul, the images might reflect a specific realm's unique attributes or characteristics.

3. **Images projected through an orb?** Orbs are often interpreted in spiritual contexts as vehicles or manifestations of energy. Suppose orbs are featured in the images or videos you're referring to. In that case, they could visualize how souls or spiritual energies travel or communicate across different realms.
4. **Some images of Heaven?** The depictions could indeed be artists' or visionaries' interpretations of what they perceive heaven or higher spiritual realms to be like. The individual's cultural, religious, and personal beliefs about the afterlife often influence these interpretations.
5. **Who are the creatures escorting the souls of animals?** The entities you're referring to could be spiritual guides, angels, midway creatures, or any celestial being designated to assist souls in transitioning from one realm to another. In various spiritual traditions, there are angels, spirit guides, or other entities who help guide souls, including those of animals, ensuring they reach their appropriate destination in the afterlife. These concepts can vary widely across different cultures and belief systems, and the images or descriptions might be symbolic, attempting to convey aspects of the afterlife that are beyond our typical understanding or perception. The idea that animals are escorted and cared for suggests a belief system that recognizes a continuation of the soul's journey for all living beings, not just humans.

What Have We Learned?

In conclusion, our journey through the profound questions surrounding what happens after we die has taken us across a landscape rich with near-death experiences, the structured stages of the afterlife, and the nuanced concepts of heaven and hell. We've explored the intriguing notion that our beloved animals also partake in an afterlife journey, reuniting with us and their kind in a realm free from earthly constraints.

Through the accounts of near-death experiences, we've glimpsed the potential stages that souls encounter beyond the physical realm, offering a preview of the afterlife's transformative potential. These personal accounts and various cultural and spiritual teachings suggest a journey of progression, learning, and eventual reunification with the universe's fundamental essence.

Heaven and hell have been examined not as final destinations but as states reflective of our soul's journey and alignment with universal love and knowledge. The idea that animals share in this journey broadens our understanding of the afterlife, suggesting a universe where all forms of consciousness continue to evolve and interconnect.

Our exploration has also touched on the choices that await us after death – the decision to move towards the light, the opportunity for soul growth, and the potential to connect with loved ones. These choices underscore the afterlife as a dynamic continuation of our soul's journey, offering further opportunities for growth and enlightenment.

Interpreting the images and messages received through photographs, videos, visions, dreams, or other means provides us with a language to understand the afterlife's nuances. These symbols and signs, often delivered in moments of deep reflection or through the lens of a camera, invite us to consider the interconnectedness of all things and the ongoing presence of those who have passed.

As we close this chapter, we're reminded that the journey after death is as rich and complex as life, woven with opportunities for learning, evolution, and love. While the mystery of what happens after we die remains partially veiled, the insights gathered from near-death experiences, spiritual teachings, and personal reflections offer comforting and inspiring glimpses into the continuum of existence. In this grand cosmic journey, our connections to each other, the universe, and the essence of love persist and evolve, guiding us toward a deeper understanding of life, death, and the profound journey that lies beyond.

Chapter 8

Angels, Spirit Guides & Mystical Beings

We are not separate from the events of our world. We are not separate from one another. We are not separate from the earth, and we are not separate from the heavens.
Gregg Braden, author of The Divine Matrix

There are kind-hearted spirits and souls, who have once lived on Earth and passed away, and then come back to help and guide us. Sometimes, we might have known these souls in our past lives. We call them angels and spirit guides. These guides offer us their wisdom and support, helping us navigate our lives on Earth. They act as a connection between our world and the spiritual realm, providing us with advice, comfort, and direction. Even though we can't see them, they are always there, gently pushing us to grow and showing us the right path. By learning more about these spiritual entities, we start to understand how deeply connected we are with them, and how they play a significant role in guiding and protecting us throughout our lives.

Angels

There are various types of angels, each with their own unique domain. For example, there are angels dedicated to music, others who watch over animals, and those who are connected to nature. During the time of writing this book, a hawk flew right in front of my car and lingered there momentarily before flying off. These occurrences suggest that angels are at work, orchestrating events around us, often in ways that might seem coincidental but are actually signs or messages.

In our everyday lives, when we encounter something unusual or serendipitous, it's often angels working behind the scenes. I believe that they are not just random happenings but celestial beings working to guide or communicate with us. The communication is more of a connection through our inner thoughts and feelings. They guide us subtly, responding to our intentions and questions, often in ways that require our trust and attentiveness to perceive.

Over thousands of years, the way people see angels has changed a lot. The word "angel" comes from a Greek word that means "messenger," which fits perfectly because, throughout history and in many stories, angels are seen as messengers from a divine place, bringing important news and offering guidance and help to those who need it.

Today, many people from different cultures and backgrounds think of angels as kind, helpful forces in the universe that anyone can reach out to for guidance and protection. They are also seen as caring companions and protectors who help people through tough times.

People often turn to angels when they're feeling unsure or worried, looking for a glimmer of hope or a boost of strength. The help from angels isn't always about grand gestures; it's more about the little signs, gut feelings, or happy coincidences that seem to suggest an angel's touch.

The fascination with angels reflects a deep human wish to connect with something bigger than ourselves, to feel supported by a kind and wise presence, and to tap into a deeper understanding that's believed to exist in the spiritual realm. As people and societies grow and change, so does our understanding of angels. This ongoing interest shows our collective hope, curiosity, and desire to find deeper meaning in our lives.

I obviously believe deeply in the presence and guidance of angels in our lives. I feel their presence many, many times, especially during significant moments. I know that the instances when Boo Boo got lost, angels were there to protect her, aware of her crucial role in my life and mission.

In the spiritual hierarchy, angels and archangels serve distinct yet interconnected roles. Archangels, known for their immense power and relatively fewer numbers, are pivotal in the cosmic order, involved in high-level decisions about the soul's journey post-death. Angels, on the other hand, are closely connected to Earth, offering guidance and support to its inhabitants. They assist in the transition of souls, working with midway creatures to aid our spiritual journey. My encounters with these beings, documented through numerous photographs, affirm their active engagement in our lives.

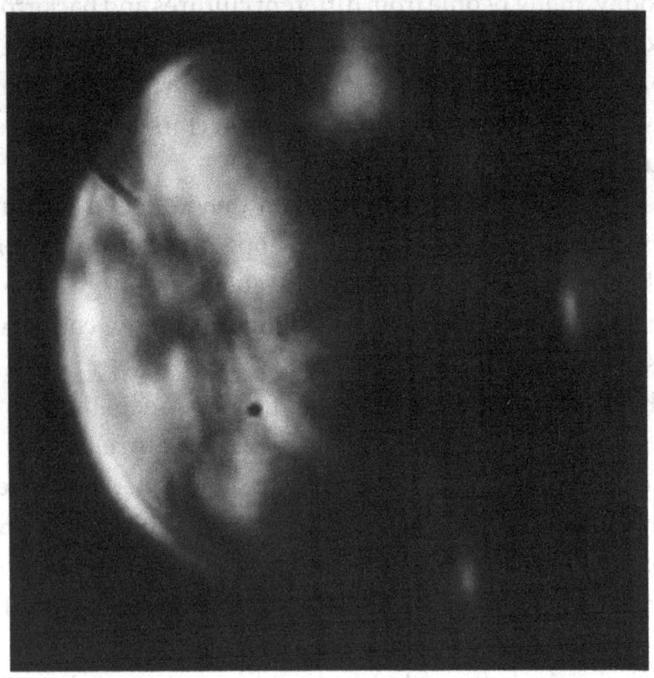

Archangel unidentified.

My desire to understand life beyond death was one of the catalysts that led me to explore various aspects of the spirit realm. I have always been intrigued by the roles of spirit guides and the impact of meditation and clairvoyance. Interactions with seasoned lightworkers and experiences of divine communication have reinforced my belief in the potent assistance we receive from the spiritual realm. Experiences with my seraphim angels, personal guardians through life's journey, have been particularly transformative, revealing the depth of love and support extended to us from the spiritual world. This realization brings immense comfort and eradicates the fear of death, emphasizing the unending support and love we receive from beyond.

The intricate organization of the spiritual realm, with its various classes of angels and their specific duties, underscores a complex yet beautifully orchestrated universe. From the protective and communicative roles of archangels to the guiding presence of guardian angels and spirit guides, the celestial hierarchy is designed to assist and guide us on our spiritual and earthly paths.

My experiences and the shared beliefs of many others highlight a universe teeming with divine support, where angels, archangels, and other celestial beings play vital roles in our lives, guiding, protecting, and inspiring us toward our highest potential.

The profound lesson that emerges from these experiences is the realization of an immense, almost unfathomable love that envelops you. This love is not superficial or fleeting; it's deep, enduring, and originates from various benevolent entities in the universe that are tirelessly working in your favor, championing your cause, and guiding your path.

For anyone struggling with self-doubt, feeling unworthy, or grappling with challenges in life or love, grasp this truth:

you are cherished immeasurably by forces greater than you can comprehend. The spiritual realm, though unseen, is profoundly invested in your well-being and happiness. This might seem too good to be true, almost like a fanciful notion, but it's a reality that transcends our ordinary understanding of love and support.

The message is clear and profoundly uplifting: you are enveloped in a love so vast and deep it transcends human understanding. This love is eternal, unwavering, and available to you at every moment of your existence. Embrace this truth, let it fortify your spirit, and allow it to illuminate your path with hope, courage, and a deep sense of belonging in the universe.

Calling All Angels

Interpreting messages from angels involves a combination of intuition, openness, and discernment, as angelic guidance can be subtle and symbolic. Here are some steps and tips to help you interpret messages from angels:

1. **Be Open to Receive:** Cultivate a mindset of openness and receptivity. Angels can send messages in various forms, so it's essential to be open to receiving guidance in unexpected ways.
2. **Create a Conducive Environment:** Find a quiet space where you can relax and be undisturbed. Meditation or prayer can help calm your mind and raise your vibrational energy, making it easier to connect with angelic beings.
3. **Ask for Guidance:** If you seek answers or assistance, ask the angels for help. Be specific about what you need guidance on but remain open to the form the answer may take.
4. **Notice Signs and Symbols:** Angels often communicate through signs, symbols, or synchronicities. Common signs include feathers, repeating number sequences (like

111 or 444), flashes of light, or unexpected encounters with animals or objects.

5. **Pay Attention to Your Intuition:** Your intuition is a powerful tool for receiving and interpreting angelic messages. Trust your gut feelings, the sudden insights, or the "knowing" that comes without logical explanation.
6. **Interpret Your Dreams:** Angels may communicate through dreams, as this is a time when your conscious mind is at rest and more receptive to subtle energies. Keep a journal by your bed to record any significant dreams or symbols you encounter.
7. **Seek Confirmation:** If you receive a message but are unsure of its interpretation, ask the angels for clarification or confirmation. They are happy to provide further guidance to ensure their messages are understood.
8. **Use Divination Tools:** Some people find it helpful to use divination tools like angel cards or pendulums to receive and interpret messages from angels. Always approach these tools with respect and a clear intention.
9. **Be Patient:** Sometimes the message may not be immediately clear. Give it time and space, and the meaning may become apparent through additional signs or reflection.
10. **Practice Gratitude:** After receiving guidance, express gratitude to the angels for their assistance. Acknowledging their help fosters a positive connection and encourages further communication.

Remember, the key to interpreting messages from angels is to trust your inner wisdom and the feelings that accompany the signs you receive. With practice and a heartfelt intention, you can develop a more profound understanding of the messages the angels are trying to convey to you.

Archangels

Archangels are like the superheroes of the angel world, holding a special place with their amazing strength and important jobs in the universe. The name "archangel" itself tells us they're the top angels, with "arch-" meaning chief or leader.

Think of Michael, the archangel, like a brave knight, always ready to fight off darkness with his glowing sword. People see him as a protector, someone they can call on when they're facing tough times or need help fighting off negativity. Then there's Gabriel, the ultimate messenger, who acts as a bridge between the divine and us. He's known for bringing messages that can really shake things up and change lives. Today, people look to Gabriel not just for heavenly messages but also for help with clear communication and finding inspiration, whether it's for art, making big decisions, or understanding others better.

But there are more archangels out there, each with their own special role. Raphael, for example, is all about healing. He's the one people turn to when they need help, whether it's physical, emotional, or spiritual. He's like a divine doctor, offering comfort and guidance. Uriel is the archangel of wisdom and light, helping people find their way, make tough decisions, and discover deeper truths about their lives. He's like a guiding star, providing illumination and insight when things seem unclear.

Archangels don't just work on an individual level; they have a big role in the wider world, too, helping guide humanity's progress and supporting the greater good. They're considered keepers of universal truths, working quietly behind the scenes to help the world evolve and grow.

In spiritual practices, archangels are seen as powerful allies, transcending time and space to offer their help wherever it's needed. People connect with them in various ways, through prayer, meditation, or simply by thinking about them, drawing on their strength, wisdom, and compassion. In essence, archangels are the all-stars of the angelic realm, with virtues and powers that fill people with respect and admiration. Their influence is woven throughout various spiritual beliefs, where they continue to offer guidance, protection, and enlightenment, helping steer humanity toward a deeper understanding, peace, and connection with the divine.

Both angels and archangels have unique roles in the spiritual realm. They don't progress or evolve in the same way humans do because they are already in their celestial form, dedicated to assisting us and other worlds in spiritual growth and purity.

The term "archangel" might suggest that these beings are like architects, creating and overseeing the structures of the spiritual world. Their work is intricate and vast, contributing to the universe's design and its function on various levels, from our planet to the greater cosmos.

For those interested in diving deeper, the book I mentioned several times *Urantia* explores these concepts in greater detail. Published in 1955, the identities of the authors remain a mystery to this day, attributing its content to divine beings. This book offers an expansive view of the universe, detailing the roles of angels, archangels, and other spiritual entities in a grand cosmic scheme.

My Personal Experiences

Gethsemani

In 2021, I found myself with a day entirely to myself on the Sunday before the July 4th holiday. With no commitments and Denise occupied elsewhere, my destination was the Abbey at Gethsemani in a city called Trappist. It was renowned for its beauty and the contemplative life of its monks. I arrived in time to attend a chanting session in the chapel, a mesmerizing experience heightened by the acoustics of the beautiful structure. At first, I was the only visitor but the serenity was disrupted when a woman entered with a stroller. After the chanting, curiosity led me to walk over to start a conversation with her. I was surprised to discover that she was carrying her ailing dog, seeking divine intervention for his suffering.

We shared a poignant moment as I shared with her about my loss of Boo Boo. Moved by our connection, I offered her a rosary that had been blessed, hoping it would bring her and her pet comfort. I truly believe our angels orchestrated that encounter, bringing two people who could comfort each other together at the same place at the same time. Our meeting underscored for me the mysterious ways in which people are brought together at just the right moment, offering each other support and hope.

Peppermint Ice Cream

My brother Terry and I were business partners in a company called Next Staff, specializing in franchise staffing. We attended a franchise meeting in Louisville, where we met with other franchisees and the company's leaders. We met one gentleman named Cary from Kansas City.

At the meeting, Cary shared the devastating news that his only son, a high school senior, died in a car accident the month before. Moved by his story, that night, I attempted to connect spiritually with his son with the hope that I could offer some solace to his grieving parents.

In my vision, I found myself in an ice cream shop where I met a teenager who identified himself as Cary's son. He asked me to share with Cary how much he loves his parents and mentioned peppermint ice cream as a personal detail to affirm his identity.

The following day, I met with Cary and his wife to share this experience. Despite his wife's skepticism, Cary was open to the message. The mention of peppermint ice cream, his son's favorite, deeply moved them both.

Months later, Cary shared that he had begun meditating regularly and felt he had connected with his son in a dreamlike state by a lake in Kansas City, finding great comfort in these experiences.

Visual Affirmations

I've collected numerous videos and pictures of various spiritual entities. These encounters happen as a result of my reaching out to them through my meditations. They respond by appearing in my recordings at night. I often ask for guidance on personal decisions, and when I receive affirming signs, I pay attention.

In my experiences, these spiritual beings have appeared in various forms. Some look quite human, while others are a blend of human and otherworldly features, or even pure energy. One memorable figure in my videos, which I believe to be an archangel, appeared holding a lantern, symbolizing support and guidance. Another time, a silver angel holding two rods of flashing energy appeared, seeming to encourage me on a specific venture.

These beings are not only diverse in appearance but also radiate a profound sense of love, which is deeply moving and affirming. Their presence in my videos is not just a fleeting moment; it's a deeply spiritual experience that impacts me significantly, often lingering for a long time.

Church Flowers

I was gearing up for a major moment – my first big event where I planned to reveal my videos and photos of the divine beings I had captured in my backyard. It felt like the right time to see what a crowd would think of my mystical backyard visitors. To get ready, I made it a point to visit Caldwell Chapel at the Louisville Seminary campus every day at 3:00 p.m. I was there to practice my speech with a live mic, aiming to polish it to perfection.

The day before the event, I went in for my last practice session. But as I walked through the chapel doors and down the aisle, an incredible thing happened — I was hit by the overwhelming scent of flowers. It was as if a million flowers were right there with me, even though there wasn't a single one in sight. I know this wasn't just any fragrance; it was a profound message from the angels. They were sending me a wave of love and encouragement, supporting my courage to share something that might stir up controversy. It was a moment I'll never forget, a clear sign that I wasn't alone on this journey.

Spirit Guides

My journey into understanding the spiritual realm was deeply influenced by my spirit guides. They've gently led me down a path of discovery, revealing new gifts and experiences only when I was ready to embrace them. These guides are souls who have passed on and are progressing through their own spiritual journeys, assisting people on Earth as part of their development. Often, there's a past life connection between the guide and the person they're assisting.

While guardian angels are constant companions throughout our lives, spirit guides come and go. Ramtha, one of my spirit guides with a warrior's presence, has been helping me understand how to use my gifts to spread love and positivity daily.

This guidance isn't just about grand gestures but also about the subtle ways we can positively influence others. Just like a recent encounter I had, where a friend mentioned feeling uplifted in my presence — I thought to myself, great, I'm doing it. And we can all do it; we can all make a difference. When my father was dying, he was scared, so I started showing him my pictures and videos and told him more about what happens when we die. As the time grew closer to his death, I could see that he was much more relaxed and comfortable about his passing, and actually looking forward to seeing his deceased relatives on the other side. The day he passed his last words to me were that he could see his deceased brother and sisters waiting for him.

During a meditation class led by Rhonda, I was joined by two experienced clairvoyants. One of them was named Jennifer and the other Shera. Jennifer was an old soul with a unique role in the spiritual world, battling dark forces in her visionary experiences. During this meeting, Jennifer recognized my potential, describing me as a "powerful being" of purity. Although I initially brushed off her words, I've come to see their significance as I've advanced on my spiritual path.

During our sessions, Rhonda would guide me through meditations, encouraging me to visualize and connect with my spiritual guides. She introduced me to the concept of having a variety of guides, each with a unique role, such as a guide of pleasure and a master teacher. Intriguingly, without revealing our visions to each other initially, Rhonda and I would often discover we had visualized the same guide, affirming our spiritual connection and the presence of these guides in our lives.

One such guide we identified was Zalzar, a name that surfaced not from our creation but as his true identity. Zalzar, a master teacher guide, played a significant role in my past life as my father, with Rhonda and I as his children somewhere in the Mediterranean. Our connection spanned lifetimes, from a familial bond by the ocean to adventures sailing to Greece.

Following Zalzar, I encountered Carol, embodying joy, pleasure, and a sense of twin flame connection. Alongside her, my two guardian seraphim angels, Soss and Otta, signify my progress on the ascension path. Carol's presence has been motivational, appearing in visions and even a video, holding a lantern, indicating her significant role in my spiritual journey.

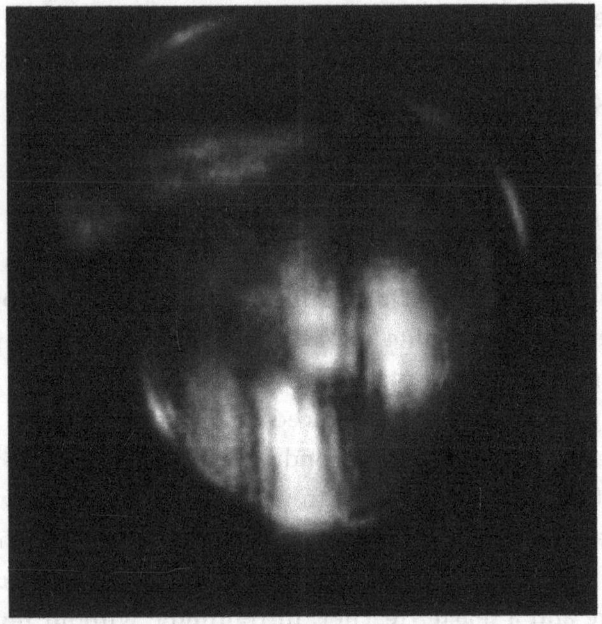

Soss and Otta can be seen on the top of the image, and there are two other seraphim angels on the bottom.

However, my visions have become less frequent, a change that both puzzles and disheartens me. These visions were a vital part of my spiritual development, offering glimpses into past lives and the wisdom of my guides.

In addition to Carol, I've been guided by Danny, a business-minded guide with an English demeanor, and Dalsaya, an Indian guide and my mother in a past life, who has been particularly present during significant business transactions.

Patty, a health guide, has also been instrumental, emphasizing that different guides appear at various stages of our spiritual journey, each bringing unique insights and support.

The spiritual path is dynamic, with guides like Dalsaya and others coming in and out of my life, each contributing to my growth and understanding. These guides, from joy and pleasure to protection and teaching, form a team that assists me in navigating life's challenges and opportunities.

Reflecting on these experiences, I'm reminded of the importance of connecting with these guides, acknowledging their presence even when direct communication seems elusive. They are always working in our favor, attempting to guide us, even when we're not actively seeking their input.

This journey has reinforced my belief in the guidance and love provided by the universe, manifested through the myriad spirit guides and angelic beings accompanying us. As I continue to explore and document my experiences, I'm reminded of the profound support system available to us, urging us to remain open and receptive to the messages and guidance they offer.

I reach out to my spirit guides for assistance in various areas of my life, whether it's financial advice or health-related concerns. If you consistently ask for their help and stay attentive, they will respond. Their responses might come in different forms – a sudden flash of light, a thought that pops into your mind, or even a vision.

To effectively communicate with your guides, it's essential to connect your consciousness with theirs. Try giving them names to strengthen this bond. Start with one, and every few weeks, you can introduce another. This naming process helps in focusing your connection and making the communication more tangible.

If you're ever unsure about a message, ask your guides to clarify it for you in a dream or through words, and pay attention to the insights you receive upon waking. While I've generally received answers, I'm currently puzzled by a spirit appearing in my videos. I initially thought he resembled Gandhi or a Mohawk Native American, but neither matched. Suddenly, just two nights ago, the Holy

Ones granted me a vision that clarified everything. They revealed the same figure I had seen before, this time guiding souls through his head. It was an eye-opening moment! This being wasn't just a spirit guide; he was a high-ranking angelic entity, deeply involved in overseeing the midwayers and the process of soul ascension. The Holy Ones showed me a graphic example of his duties to help me discern who it was and give me a clear understanding of his responsibilities, and his true nature.

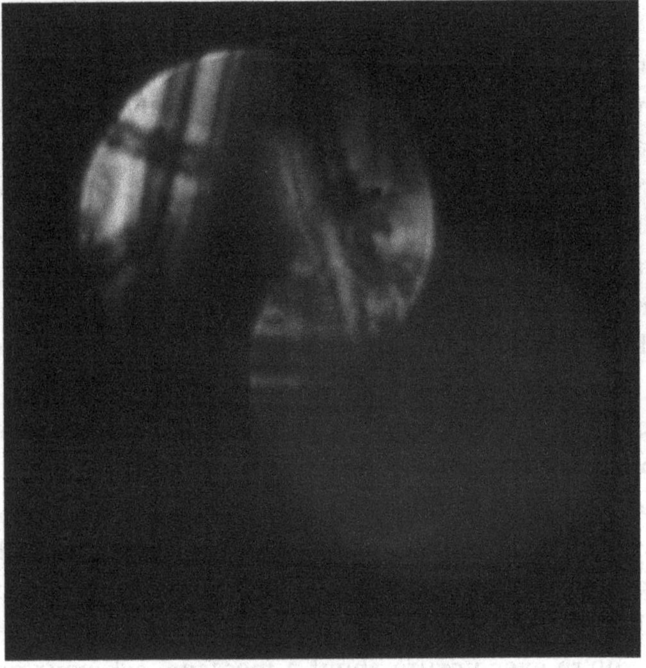

My favorite — Angel holding golden rods. This is only the second time I saw an angel through one of my videos, and she is giving me the thumbs up to move forward with building my resort.

Exploring the identities of your spirit guides can be an intriguing journey. Resources like Barbara Y. Martin and Dimitri

Moraitis's *Communing with the Divine: A Clairvoyant's Guide to Angels, Archangels, and the Spiritual Hierarchy*; Sonia Choquette's *Ask Your Guides*; and *Meet Your Guides: Embracing Your Angels, Archangels, and Ascended Masters* by Deborah Sudarsky, provide an excellent foundation for embarking on your personal exploration.

Remember, your guides are always there, assisting you, even when you're not actively reaching out to them. The more you tune in and acknowledge their presence, the more guidance and support you'll receive.

Where Do I Start?

When you're ready to start connecting with your spirit guides, it's beneficial to start with a meditation practice focusing on one guide at a time. Begin by expressing your intention to meet your guide, who could be a teaching guide, spiritual mentor, or whatever term resonates with you. During meditation, when your mind is calm, contemplate a name that naturally comes to you for this guide. You can use a pendulum to help confirm if the name you've thought of aligns with your guide. Over the next few days, seek further validation through visions or words that might come to you, either at night or during your day-to-day activities.

Once you feel connected with one guide, visualize this entity, engage with him or her, and then gradually introduce yourself to other guides. These spirit guides often vary, entering and exiting your life as needed. For instance, I recently connected with a guide who shared profound insights with me; he appeared as a dark-skinned individual in armor, reminiscent of someone from the era of the South American conquistadors. Throughout the years, I have had over 25 guides help me at one time or another.

Do We Have Free Will?

The concept of free will is a fascinating topic, especially when we think about how it operates on Earth. Our planet is unique because it gives us the ability to make choices, both good and bad. This capacity for choice is what brings about the mix of positivity and negativity we see around us.

The story of Lucifer, a high-ranking celestial figure who chose to rebel, serves as a powerful example that decisions have significant outcomes, affecting not just the physical world but also the spiritual realm. His rebellion is a reminder that our choices can have far-reaching implications beyond what we can see.

The way we're raised and the environment we grow up in heavily influence the decisions we make. Everything from family relationships to social conditions can steer us in various directions. However, there's always room for growth and improvement. Despite the factors that shape us, we all have the potential to evolve and choose a path that leads to a higher, more loving state of being.

Mystical Beings

Having explored the realm of angels and spirit guides, let's now broaden our horizons to the diverse world of mystical creatures that span various cultures and spiritual traditions. These intriguing entities are not limited to the familiar spirits and angels but encompass a wide array of beings with roles that vary from guardians to mentors, and even mischievous tricksters. Each of these beings, steeped in the stories and folklore of different societies, bring a unique flavor to the intricacies of the mystical world.

1. **Deities:** Many cultures have their own sets of gods and goddesses who interact with humans, offering help, blessings, or life lessons. These divine beings represent

different parts of nature and human life and are central figures in many global myths.

2. **Elementals:** These spirits are linked to the four classic elements – earth, air, fire, and water. For example, gnomes are connected to earth, sylphs to air, salamanders to fire, and undines or nymphs to water. People often see them as guardians of nature.
3. **Fairies:** This group includes various magical beings like pixies, leprechauns, and elves. Connected closely to nature, fairies have magical powers and play significant roles in European folklore, sometimes helping or misleading humans.
4. **Djinn or Genies:** Coming from Middle Eastern and Islamic stories, djinn live in a world parallel to ours. They can be good, bad, or neutral, have magical powers, and are famous for granting wishes, especially in Western tales.
5. **Dragons:** Seen as mystical creatures in many cultures, dragons are powerful and wise. Western stories often depict them as hoarders of treasure or great challenges, while in Eastern traditions, like in China, dragons symbolize power, strength, and luck.
6. **Ancestors:** In many native and shamanic cultures, ancestors are more than just family members who have passed away; they're seen as powerful spiritual figures who provide guidance, protection, and wisdom.
7. **Ascended Masters:** These are people who have reached a high spiritual level and help guide humanity. Famous examples include Jesus, Buddha, and Krishna.
8. **Nature Spirits:** Beyond elementals, many traditions believe in spirits that live in natural things like trees, rivers, and mountains, and even stars and planets. These spirits are respected and seen as crucial to the health of their environment.

9. **Tulpas:** This idea comes from Tibetan Buddhism and describes beings brought to life through spiritual or mental focus. These days, it is a concept in the occult and paranormal, suggesting that strong belief can create a conscious entity.
10. **Cryptids:** Typically, part of cryptozoology, creatures like Bigfoot or the Loch Ness Monster tap into the mystical side of our imagination, embodying the mysteries and potential undiscovered beings sharing our world.

What Is a Mystic?

A mystic is a person who seeks to achieve a direct, personal connection with the divine or the ultimate reality, often through experiences that transcend ordinary human comprehension. Mystics typically focus on inner, spiritual experiences, aiming to discover deeper truths about existence and the nature of the divine. They often practice meditation, contemplation, and other forms of spiritual discipline to cultivate these profound experiences.

Mysticism is not confined to a single religious or spiritual tradition; it's found across various cultures and religious frameworks, each with its own unique practices and beliefs. Whether through profound meditation, prayer, or other means, mystics strive for an experiential knowledge of the sacred, seeking a sense of unity with the universe or a profound understanding of the nature of reality. Their journey is deeply personal, often characterized by moments of enlightenment, insight, and a deep sense of connectedness with all things. My journey to recognizing myself as a mystic was marked by the sequence of deeply personal experiences I have described; uncovering the Healing Mary, my discovery of orbs and delving into their contents, and the initial visions that visited me in the night.

We Are All Connected

The notion that every person on Earth is interconnected gains intense clarity when we delve into the concepts presented by Gregg Braden, especially his insights on the divine matrix and quantum physics, like the idea of being in two places at once. This interconnectedness isn't just a spiritual belief but is backed by scientific exploration, suggesting a deep, underlying unity among all of us.

While we navigate our lives in the third dimension, there's a growing understanding and movement towards higher dimensions – such as the fourth and fifth – where interactions with more refined spiritual entities like angels and archangels become more tangible. These higher beings fine-tune their vibrations to communicate with us, offering guidance and insights.

The thread that weaves us all together is a universal consciousness, a vast, accessible field where knowledge and wisdom flow freely, available to anyone who seeks it, whether consciously or in the depths of the subconscious. In my own practice, meditation serves as a bridge to this universal consciousness, allowing for direct communication with spiritual guides and angels, especially during the quiet of the night. These interactions often come through visions or messages that guide my personal journey.

This interconnectedness isn't confined to extraordinary spiritual encounters; it permeates every aspect of our lives, influencing even the most ordinary moments. Have you ever felt an unexplained connection with someone you've just met in an everyday place, like a supermarket? Such instances hint at the underlying unity that connects us all.

Peeling away the layers of ego and societal expectations to embrace our true spiritual essence – characterized by light, love, and purity – allows us to experience this interconnectedness on a profound level. In this state, free from ego's constraints, we embody the virtues of love, compassion, and spiritual clarity.

Such insights also offer a perspective on the afterlife, echoing accounts from those who have experienced near-death phenomena, where love is a recurring theme. They suggest that shedding our ego and the superficial identities we cling to can reveal our true nature, one that is inherently pure, loving, and deeply connected to all life.

My Spirit Guides

I want to extend my deepest gratitude to my personal spirit guides, who have been my unwavering sources of guidance, comfort, and insight. Your presence in my life has been a beacon of light, guiding me through life's twists and turns with an invisible, yet dearly felt, touch. Thank you for your ceaseless support, for the gentle nudges towards growth, and for the infinite wisdom you impart in the quiet moments of reflection.

Your guidance is a gift that has enriched my journey, helping me to navigate the complexities of life with a deeper sense of clarity and purpose. I am profoundly grateful for your constant companionship, your boundless patience, and the unconditional love you shower upon me, even when I am least aware of it. Your presence is a constant reminder of the interconnectedness of all things and the ever-present support available to us from the unseen realms. My heartfelt thanks to:

Master Babaji	Vahaundress	Amira
Emera	Markella	Justin
Barbeil	Gersia	Penta
Hera	Chastaine	Ramtha
Lord Hastein	Thalie	Carol
Chamuel	Mona Swayo	Dalsaya
Lauviah	Crying Wolf	Necatarian

St. Cecilia	Tula
Tabitha	Thaddeus
Octavio	Calmere
Esterra	Mehela
Darius	Patty
Zalzar	Danny

Chapter 9

Meditation & Manifestation

A grateful mind is a great mind which eventually attracts to itself great things.

Plato

Embarking on my path to becoming a student, and eventually a mindfulness teacher, has been a transformative experience. Mindfulness is the practice of being fully present and engaged at the moment, aware of your thoughts, feelings, bodily sensations, and surrounding environment without judgment. It involves acknowledging your thoughts and feelings without getting caught up in them or allowing them to dictate your reactions. By fostering mindfulness, individuals can experience reduced stress, enhanced emotional regulation, improved concentration, and greater well-being.

When I discovered the statue of Mary, I found the Earth and Spirit Center simultaneously. I genuinely believe that I discovered Mary when I did because I was finally at a place in my life to be open to the Center and searching for it. My connection to the place deepened when I attended a wine and cheese reception for visiting dignitaries Di Anne and Tom Kerrigan. They had accepted a post to teach mindfulness and meditation at the Center. We connected instantly, and they suggested that I enroll in the classes they offered called Meditation 1 and 2.

Following these courses and forging a strong bond with Tom, I was invited to collaborate on an exciting initiative for the Urban League called KY Builds. To date, we have taught mindfulness and meditation to over 600 students.

Reflecting on this journey, I recognize how the Holy Ones sparked my interest in spirituality, guiding me through a series of books, serendipitous encounters, unusual circumstances, visions, and out-of-body experiences. This path was about learning, opening doors to new opportunities, and deepening my connection to the celestial realm and the Holy Ones. My migration from student to teacher has been about personal growth and sharing the gift of mindfulness with others, creating a ripple effect of positivity and spiritual awakening.

Meditation

In our society, structured over millennia to prioritize and glorify the ego, we find ourselves enveloped in a culture that measures worth through material possessions and status symbols – our cars, homes, and various coveted objects. This cultural backdrop, intertwined with the values instilled in us from childhood, shapes our aspirations and decisions, often anchoring them in egocentric objectives.

Yet, amidst this ego-driven existence, a profound practice – meditation – offers a gateway to transcendence. Beginning your explorations into meditation and mindfulness may seem daunting in our fast-paced lives, where finding a moment of peace can be a challenge. However, the beauty of mindfulness is its accessibility; it can be integrated into our daily routines, offering a respite from the relentless pace of life.

Meditation is not just a practice but a profound connection to our higher selves, an innate aspect of our being that yearns for acknowledgement and unity with a greater existence beyond the material. This pursuit starkly contrasts our world's ego-driven values, making the development of a consistent meditation practice a challenging yet rewarding endeavor.

Through meditation, we tap into the core of our being, where decisions stem from a place of love and compassion.

This alignment facilitates a deeper connection with our higher selves. It influences our actions in the world, contributing to our karmic journey — a journey we navigate through countless lifetimes, constantly evolving and learning.

Meditation is a transformative portal, offering experiences that imbue us with peace, joy, and a profound sense of interconnectedness. These experiences diminish the allure of materialistic pursuits, shifting our focus to the essence of existence and the profound pleasure of spiritual awakening.

While it is natural to appreciate material comforts, the essence of meditation lies in transcending these attachments to foster a deeper sense of purpose and fulfillment. Establishing a meditation practice amidst our busy lives may require effort. Still, it is an investment that yields profound spiritual dividends.

As we navigate our earthly journey, every moment dedicated to meditation enriches our soul, preparing us for the continuous voyage of learning and evolution in the cosmos. The universe, with its infinite complexity and multitude of entities, offers limitless opportunities for growth and understanding. Meditation is the key that unlocks these doors, enabling us to delve deeper into the mysteries of existence and progress on our eternal path of enlightenment.

One crucial aspect I want to emphasize is the value of meditation and an essential insight shared by the Holy Ones. It's a common misconception that profound spiritual development requires withdrawing from the world, perhaps retreating to a monastery or spending decades in remote, ascetic solitude. Many, including myself, have pondered whether actual spiritual growth is out of reach without such extreme measures — without venturing to Tibet, traversing the Himalayas in search of Shangri-La, or abandoning worldly life for sequestered spiritual practice.

However, the Holy Ones clarify this misconception. They assert that retreating from the world isn't necessary for everyone. Indeed, some individuals might choose monastic life or seclusion, not purely for spiritual enlightenment but to escape worldly existence's complexities.

Contrary to the notion that spiritual growth requires isolation, the Holy Ones emphasize the importance of engaging with life's full spectrum. They encourage living amidst society, embracing experiences, nurturing families, and participating in communal living. This involvement in the world isn't a barrier to spiritual development; instead, it's a fertile ground for growth, offering many opportunities for learning, loving, and spiritually evolving.

Meditation offers a sanctuary within the whirlwind of life's challenges. It is accessible to all, anytime and anywhere, except during activities like driving, where full attention is necessary. This practice is a versatile ally in managing the stress and tribulations inherent in our existence, demonstrating that spiritual growth doesn't require isolation in monasteries or distant lands.

Furthermore, the accumulation of academic accolades and intellectual achievements holds little significance in the eyes of the Holy Ones. They remain indifferent to the number of books one has read, the degrees one has earned, or the prestige of educational institutions attended. Instead, the accurate measure of spiritual progress in their eyes is rooted in love, compassion, dedication, integrity, and respect for oneself and others. These virtues truly matter and pave the way for advancement in the spiritual realm. It's a reminder that our actions, our capacity to love, and our commitment to doing what is right are the cornerstones of meaningful spiritual development.

Meditation for Self-Discovery

Oneness refers to a state of being in which an individual experiences a deep sense of harmony and alignment between their mind, body, and spirit. It's a profound connection where the usual boundaries that separate different aspects of the self, dissolve, leading to complete integration and unity. This state is characterized by a fundamental understanding and acceptance of oneself, transcending internal conflicts, doubts, and fragmentation. People who achieve oneness often report a heightened sense of self-awareness, inner peace, and a deep, intuitive understanding of their true nature and purpose in life.

Meditation, as a form of being one with yourself, emphasizes self-awareness, self-acceptance, and inner harmony. This approach to meditation encourages individuals to delve deeply into their own minds and hearts, fostering a sense of unity and connection with their innermost selves. Here's a closer look at how meditation facilitates this impactful self-union:

1. **Self-Awareness:** Meditation is a vital tool for enhancing self-awareness. By sitting in silence and observing one's thoughts and feelings without judgment, practitioners can develop a deeper understanding of their mental patterns, emotional responses, and underlying beliefs. This heightened awareness allows individuals to recognize aspects of themselves that they might typically overlook or avoid, facilitating a more comprehensive sense of self.
2. **Acknowledging the Inner Self:** Through meditation, individuals learn to acknowledge all parts of themselves, including their strengths, weaknesses, joys, and sorrows. This acknowledgement is not about striving for change or improvement but about accepting oneself fully in the present moment. Such acceptance is crucial to achieving a state of oneness.
3. **Finding Inner Peace:** Consistent meditation can lead to true inner peace. By regularly centering oneself and calming the mind, individuals can cultivate a serenity that transcends external circumstances. This inner peace

is key to feeling unified with oneself, as it signifies harmony between the mind, body, and spirit.

4. **Self-Compassion:** Meditation fosters self-compassion, encouraging individuals to treat themselves with kindness and understanding. Recognizing one's common humanity and offering oneself the same compassion extended to others is vital for feeling connected and at one with oneself.
5. **Enhancing Mind-Body Connection:** Meditation strengthens the connection between mind and body. By focusing on the breath or engaging in mindful movements, individuals become more attuned to their physical selves, recognizing the interdependence of physical and mental well-being.
6. **Cultivating Authenticity:** Being one with oneself through meditation involves embracing authenticity. This practice encourages individuals to strip away external influences and societal expectations, allowing their true selves to emerge. In doing so, they can live more authentically, making choices and taking actions that align with their inner truth.
7. **Spiritual Connection:** For many, achieving oneness through meditation is also a spiritual journey. It involves connecting with a deeper, more universal aspect of oneself, sometimes described as the soul or higher self. This connection can provide a sense of purpose, direction, and belonging.

Meditating as a form of being one with yourself is about cultivating a deep, intimate relationship with your inner being. It's a journey of exploration, acceptance, and unity, where the barriers between different facets of oneself dissolve, leading to a harmonious and integrated existence.

Meditation to Communicate with the Other Realm

Meditating to connect to the spirit world is an ancient and sacred art that has been a cornerstone of numerous spiritual traditions. Meditation can be harnessed as a powerful tool for those seeking to deepen their connection with the unseen forces that pervade our universe. Here's an overview of how meditation is believed to facilitate communication with the spirit realm:

1. **Meditation as a Tool for Altered States of Consciousness:** Meditation is known for altering one's state of consciousness. By quieting the mind and focusing inward, practitioners can reach consciousness states different from the usual waking state. In these altered states, individuals may become more receptive to nonphysical realities or entities.
2. **Enhanced Intuition and Psychic Abilities:** Regular meditation is often associated with heightened intuition and the development of psychic abilities such as clairvoyance (extrasensory), clairaudience (supernatural), and clairsentience (intuitiveness). These abilities facilitate perception beyond the physical senses, allowing individuals to receive messages or insights from the spirit world.
3. **Creating a Sacred Space:** Meditation often involves creating a mental or physical space conducive to spiritual or metaphysical experiences. This space is considered safe and sacred for connecting with spiritual entities or energies.
4. **Intention and Focus:** Setting a clear intention is crucial to communicating with spirits through meditation. Practitioners often focus on making contact with the spirit realm or specific entities, guiding their meditation toward this purpose.

5. **Protection and Grounding:** Engaging with the spirit world through meditation typically involves protection and grounding practices. Meditators often visualize protective barriers or use grounding techniques to ensure their experiences are safe and anchored in their physical well-being.
6. **Interpretation and Discernment:** Experiences of communicating with spirits through meditation can be subtle and open to interpretation. Individuals often need to develop skills in discernment to understand and integrate the information or messages received.
7. **Spiritual and Cultural Context:** Meditating to communicate with spirits is deeply rooted in various cultural and spiritual traditions. The understanding and approach to these interactions can vary significantly, influenced by one's cultural background and spiritual beliefs.

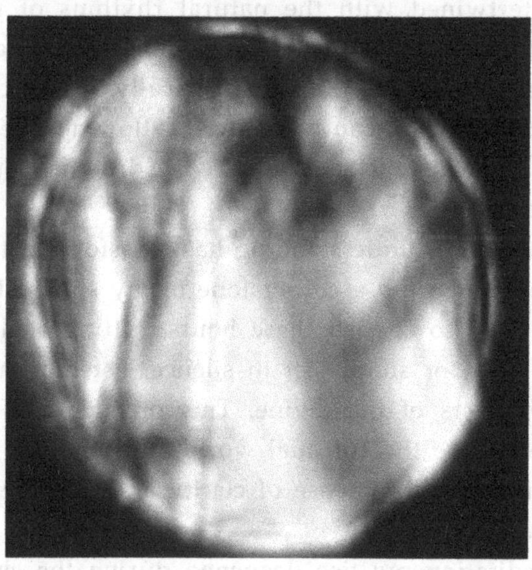

Master Babaji – I was reading about Master Babaji during my daily meditation and as always, the seraphim arranged for him to be present that night! He's on the far left.

As discussed briefly before, the early hours of the day, such as between 2 a.m. and 3 a.m., hold a special significance for those seeking to connect with the spiritual realm. This time is often described as a prime window for spiritual communication, when the boundaries separating our world from the others become exceptionally permeable, allowing for a seamless flow of celestial wisdom.

During these early hours, the hustle and bustle of daily life come to a standstill and the clamor of the physical world gradually fades into tranquil silence. It's as if the universe itself pauses, creating a serene backdrop perfect for tuning into the subtle frequencies of the divine. This quietude is not just the absence of noise but a profound presence of peace, making it an ideal setting for the mind to become more receptive to spiritual messages.

The tranquility of this time is not merely coincidental but deeply intertwined with the natural rhythms of the Earth and the human body. In these moments, as the rest of the world sleeps, the distractions that typically occupy our minds and hearts are significantly reduced, allowing our spiritual antennas to pick up signals otherwise drowned out by the day's chaos.

Embracing this understanding has transformed this early-morning window into a cornerstone of my spiritual practice. I have learned to cherish these hours, setting aside time to meditate, pray, or simply sit in silence, listening attentively for the whispers of the divine. This practice has deepened my connection to the spiritual world and enriched my daily life, infusing it with a sense of clarity and purpose that was previously elusive.

My meditation practice deepened during the challenging time of COVID. I would seek refuge in meditating after a long day of work. As we all know, many places were closed.

Luckily, my chapel was open during online classes, providing a sanctuary for my daily habits.

Through meditation and reading, guided by the Holy Ones, I've been led down a path of continuous learning and spiritual growth. My journey involved questioning, seeking, and receiving answers, often through the mystical images captured in my videos. One notable instance was when I requested to see an angel. The universe responded with a striking image that defied conventional expectations, offering a unique glimpse into the celestial realm.

Through this, I've come to appreciate the truth that communication with the divine is not bound by time and space constraints as we understand them. Instead, it invites us into a space of openness and receptivity, where the heart and mind can align with the universe's infinite wisdom. This lesson, learned in the quiet before dawn, has illuminated my path and guided my steps on this spiritual journey.

Chakras

Chakras play a significant role in meditation practices, especially within traditions recognizing these energy centers. The idea is that focusing on and harmonizing the chakras can enhance one's meditation experience, and achieve greater balance and well-being. Here's how chakras are integrated into meditation practices:

1. **Focusing on Specific Chakras:** During meditation, individuals might focus on a specific chakra that corresponds to the area of their life or aspect of their being they wish to improve or balance. For example, someone seeking to enhance their communication skills might meditate on their throat chakra, while another person looking for more grounding might focus on the root chakra.

2. **Visualization:** Visualization is a common technique in chakra meditation. Practitioners might visualize the chakra as a spinning wheel or flower, imagining its associated color and perhaps even chanting the corresponding bija mantra (a one-syllable sound). This visualization helps to focus the mind and direct energy to the chakra, aiming to open or balance it.
3. **Breathing Techniques:** Breathwork can be integrated with chakra meditation, where breathing is focused or directed toward a particular chakra. This can help to clear blockages and stimulate the flow of energy.
4. **Balancing and Aligning Chakras:** Many meditation practices aim to balance or align all seven chakras, fostering a sense of wholeness and harmony. Meditators might go through each chakra in sequence, from the root to the crown, focusing on the attributes and health of each energy center.
5. **Physical Postures:** Certain meditation practices, especially those influenced by yoga, might incorporate specific postures or mudras (hand gestures) corresponding to different chakras, facilitating focus and energy flow to those areas.
6. **Healing and Transformation:** Individuals often seek healing or transformative experiences through chakra meditation. By focusing on and balancing their chakras, they aim to resolve emotional, physical, or spiritual issues, enhancing overall well-being.
7. **Enhanced Awareness and Insight:** By meditating on the chakras, practitioners can develop a deeper awareness of their inner world and the interplay between their physical, emotional, and spiritual selves. This heightened awareness can lead to insights and a more intimate connectivity with oneself and

the universe. In these ways, chakras are central to certain meditation practices, providing a framework for understanding and influencing the practitioner's energy and consciousness.

Chakras Overview

1. **Earth Star Chakra**: Connects us with Earth and guides our life path
2. **Root Chakra**: (Muladhara): Influences our basic survival instincts and sense of belonging
3. **Sacral Chakra**: (Svadhisthana): Governs creativity and relationships
4. **Navel Chakra**: Fosters courage and protection
5. **Solar Plexus Chakra:** (Manipura): Manages personal power and influences
6. **Heart Chakra**: (Anahata): Balances physical and spiritual love
7. **Throat Chakra**: (Vishuddha): Facilitates communication and creativity
8. **Third Eye Chakra**: (Ajna): Enhances intuition and perception
9. **Crown Chakra**: (Sahasrara): Connects to spiritual consciousness
10. **Causal Chakra**: Focuses on love and higher awareness
11. **Soul Star Chakra**: Offers soul-level insights and access to Akashic Records
12. **Divine Gateway Chakra**: Represents the ultimate spiritual connection

Manifestation

After exploring some enlightening books on the subject, manifestation is a concept that truly unfolded for me. Initially, the depth of commitment and belief required for manifesting wasn't entirely clear. It's about genuine conviction in the good and positive forces at work in the universe, channeling love and positive intent in everything you do.

Reflecting on my manifesting journey, a significant early experience dealt with the loss of my treasured Boo Boo. In my despair, I reached out to the cosmos, seeking a way to keep Boo Boo with me. This experience underscored a crucial lesson: when intentions are pure and aligned with love, the universe responds, sometimes miraculously. This was evident when I started seeing Boo Boo's face in the orbs in my yard, a comforting and mystical manifestation.

These orbs weren't limited to outdoor spaces, though. They started presenting themselves everywhere, even inside my home. They seemed to be spiritual vehicles, carrying the essence of beings close to my heart and reinforcing the power and reach of manifesting.

This path of manifesting, underpinned by the act of discernment, intuition, and a commitment to spiritual inquiry, has unveiled the underlying interconnectedness of our desires, thoughts, and the universal fabric that responds to them. From seeing Boo Boo's face in orbs to capturing unexpected divine figures in my videos, the journey has been a testament to the power of asking, believing, and receiving, anchored in the steadfast belief in the good and love that pervades the cosmos.

My search for a meditative space didn't lead me to a secluded mountaintop but to the Caldwell Chapel, as stated earlier. This was discovered not through solitude but through a series of intuitive nudges and a vivid dream. This experience revealed that spiritual guidance can manifest in myriad forms, urging us to remain open and receptive, even in our immediate surroundings. The manifestation, for me, was realized when Reverend Dr. Andrew Pomerville, the president of the Louisville Seminary, decided to give me the key to the chapel.

I have long desired to build a retreat somewhere beautiful. The Loretto Motherhouse is the traditional "home place" for the Sisters of Loretto and a spiritual center for the broader Loretto Community. My original vision saw me building the retreat there, but red tape thwarted my plans. I didn't succumb to disillusionment but stayed attuned to the universe's whispers, which eventually guided me to Taylorsville Lake. Upon setting foot on this land, I felt a deep resonance, a clear signal that this was the destined place for my spiritual and communal aspirations.

These personal journeys highlight that spiritual growth and the art of manifestation are intertwined with the day-to-day decisions of our lives. They are unique for each individual, shaped by cosmic guidance and personal intuition. By aligning our deepest intentions with the collective good and remaining open to the universe's guidance, we can traverse our spiritual path with trust and clarity, discovering real growth and fulfillment in the most unexpected places.

There's a fascinating aspect of manifestation in which we shape our reality without realizing it. Throughout our lives, we harbor hopes, dreams, and wishes. When these aspirations materialize, it's often the result of our unconscious manifestation abilities at work.

My past incarnations influenced my affinity for clear, pristine bodies of water. I know that my home in a previous life was distinguished by its crystal-clear lakes and splendid gardens, which have left a deep imprint on my soul. After my divorce in 2000, the first home I purchased had a small backyard in which I felt compelled to construct a large pond — a decision driven by an inner pull. Fast-forward to 2009, and my wife and I were considering a move. I harbored a deep-seated desire for a property with a natural water feature, like a lively spring or stream.

Remarkably, when my wife suggested we visit a particular house, the first thing that struck us wasn't the house itself but the stream gracefully meandering through the backyard — a dream realized in the form of a natural spring. This is the home where we reside today.

My yearning for a water feature was a manifestation brought to life, subtly crafted by the universe in response to my desires, even though I wasn't consciously focusing on it every day. It illustrates how our innermost wishes and dreams, even when not at the forefront of our conscious minds, are potent signals to the universe, shaping our reality in ways we might only realize in hindsight.

The Secret

Rhonda Byrne's *The Secret* is a seminal book that does a deep dive into the Law of Attraction, a principle suggesting that the universe is governed by a law that attracts like unto itself. Released in 2006, the book has since become a global phenomenon, translated into numerous languages and sparking a wave of interest in manifestation.

The Secret's core is the belief that one's thoughts can manifest reality. "Thoughts become things," Byrne proclaims. She proposes positive thoughts attract positive experiences, while negative thoughts bring undesirable outcomes. This philosophy encourages individuals to focus their mental energy on their desires, aspirations, and goals, asserting that such focus will bring those desires into reality.

Byrne outlines several critical steps for harnessing the Law of Attraction:

1. **Ask:** Clearly articulate and define what you desire. The universe needs specificity to deliver what you wish for.
2. **Believe:** Have unwavering faith that your request will manifest. Doubt is considered an obstacle to the realization of your desires.
3. **Receive:** Be open and ready to receive what the universe sends. This involves feeling as though what you've asked for is already yours and being grateful for it.

Oprah

One of the most famous stories about Oprah Winfrey and her manifestation is her experience with the movie *The Color Purple*. Oprah has often shared how she used visualization and the power of intention to manifest her role in this film, demonstrating her belief in the Law of Attraction and the power of positive thinking.

Initially captivated by Alice Walker's novel, Oprah's deep connection to the book's themes ignited a desire within her to be part of its film adaptation despite having no prior acting experience. This desire set the wheels of the universe in motion. Oprah didn't just wish to be part of the film; she embodied the role in her mind's eye, practicing the Law of Attraction by visualizing herself on set, delivering lines, and immersing herself in the character. This wasn't mere hope; it was a firm belief in the outcome, a conviction that she would be part of the movie's journey.

When the opportunity to audition arose, Oprah seized it, demonstrating the Law of Attraction's principle that action is a critical component of manifestation. Her proactive approach, combined with her unwavering belief, propelled her forward. Even when faced with uncertainty during the casting process, she maintained her focus and intention, eventually leading to a moment of surrender — a key aspect of the Law of Attraction, where one releases attachment to the outcome, trusting that the universe will deliver.

Her role as Sofia in *The Color Purple* marked a significant achievement in her career and showcased the power of combining deep desire, visualization, belief, and action with the ability to let go and trust in the universe's plan. Oprah's journey to securing her role in the film epitomizes the Law of Attraction, demonstrating that when one aligns one's energy and intention with one's desires, the universe conspires to turn those desires into reality.

Jim Carrey

In 1985, a young Jim Carrey, then only 23, boldly wrote a check to himself for $10 million, dating it a decade into the future for "acting services rendered." At this time, Carrey was just a budding actor, grappling with the uncertainties of his career, with the daunting fallback of laboring in a Canadian steel mill if his acting dreams fell through. Undeterred, he always kept that check with him, a testament to his belief in his potential.

Fast-forward ten years, and Carrey's reality had transformed dramatically. Roles in *Ace Ventura, The Mask,* and *Dumb and Dumber* catapulted him to stardom, turning the dream encapsulated by that check into reality. Jim Carrey's journey brings to light a poignant perspective on success. After achieving fame and wealth, he shared a thought-provoking insight: "Everybody should get rich and famous and do everything they ever dreamed of, so they can see that it's not the answer."

While dismissing such a statement as one a wealthy person might effortlessly make is tempting, there's a more profound truth to it — a reflection on the nature of fulfillment. His message serves as a reminder that success, when defined superficially — through wealth, fame, power, or status — can lead to what author David Brooks describes as climbing the "First Mountain." On the journey to the "Second Mountain," we discover a sense of success that is genuinely satisfying and far from hollow.

Steve Harvey

On her website, *Secrets To Manifest,* Ezriah Walker explains how Steve Harvey, the celebrated comedian, television host, and radio personality, harnessed the Law of Attraction to foster success and fulfillment in his life. The Law of Attraction has been a cornerstone in Harvey's journey, enabling him to attract his desires and achieve notable success.

Affirmations and Positive Thinking: One of Harvey's strategies involves using affirmations. He starts his day by affirming his goals and desires, channeling his energies towards financial prosperity, health, and meaningful relationships. This practice aligns his mindset with his ambitions, setting the stage for their realization.

The Role of Visualization: Beyond affirmations, Harvey employs visualization to manifest his goals. He vividly imagines living the life he yearns for, feeling the associated emotions and experiences as if they were already his reality. This process reinforces his desires and signals the universe to set the wheels of manifestation in motion.

Michael Phelps

Visualization served as a cornerstone in Michael Phelps' journey to becoming a swimming legend. Thanks to his coach, Bob Bowman, visualization was deeply intertwined with his training routine. From his early days as an energetic young swimmer, Phelps learned how to harness the power of visualization to channel his focus and energy into his performances in the pool.

Struggling with restlessness and lack of focus, Phelps was introduced to the world of relaxation and visualization by Bowman through a book on relaxation techniques given to his mother, Debbie. She would read to him, guiding him through the passages, helping him to visualize success and calm his mind. This routine didn't just relax Phelps; it allowed him to mentally rehearse his swimming, seeing himself excel in the water, sometimes even drifting off to sleep.

This visualization practice wasn't just a bedtime routine but a meticulous mental rehearsal that Phelps and Bowman integrated into his training. They didn't just visualize success; they prepared for every scenario, acknowledging that races often don't go as planned. Phelps would envision various outcomes, from the ideal race to unexpected challenges, equipping him mentally for any reality he might face in the pool.

Bowman and Phelps took visualization to an advanced level, incorporating different perspectives and engaging all senses. Phelps didn't just see himself winning; he felt the cold water, heard the starting buzzer, and experienced the race from multiple viewpoints, making the visualization as vivid and natural as possible. This comprehensive sensory engagement helped trick his brain into believing these rehearsals were real, enhancing his confidence and readiness.

For Phelps, the practice of visualization was as rigorous and essential as his physical training. By the time he stepped onto the block at major competitions, he had already "swum" the race hundreds of times in his mind. This intense mental preparation was key to his ability to perform under pressure, demonstrating that when practiced diligently, visualization is not just a supplement to physical training but a critical element of achieving excellence in sports.

It's essential to recognize that our lives are an accumulation of manifestations shaped by our intentions and thoughts. Every aspect, from our relationships to material circumstances, reflects our inner state and focus. Some even argue that our collective consciousness shapes the physical world. As stated earlier, this perspective aligns with certain philosophical views in physics.

Understanding that we play a crucial role in creating our positive and negative reality can be empowering. It underscores the importance of mindful thought and intention. To further explore these concepts, I recommend the book *Dying to be Me* by Anita Moorjani. It is a thought-provoking narrative that might provide you with deeper insights into the nature of consciousness and manifestation.

The interplay between manifestation and meditation offers a profound pathway to personal transformation and realizing one's deepest desires. Through meditation, we tap into the tranquil depths of our minds, setting a fertile ground for the seeds of our intentions to grow. Conversely, manifestation empowers us to bring these intentions to life, transforming ethereal thoughts into tangible realities.

By harmonizing the introspective focus of meditation with the proactive energy of manifestation, we unlock a powerful synergy that can elevate our lives to new heights. This chapter has explored the nuances of this dynamic interplay, illuminating how, when wielded with awareness and precision, meditation and manifestation can become potent tools for sculpting the reality we aspire to live in, guiding us toward a future aligned with our deepest aspirations and highest selves.

Chapter 10

Where Do I Go from Here?

Love is the currency of the universe.

Jeff Kober

My journey into the realms of meditation, mindfulness, and spirituality has caught many people in my circle by surprise, painting a picture of transformation that few could have anticipated. The change appears dramatic and unexpected to those who have known me for years. Tim Malone, once primarily recognized for his conventional pursuits and a memorable political stint in high school where I ran for president and faced defeat, has now embarked on a path that digs deeply into the introspective and the metaphysical.

Each week, I dedicate substantial time to exploring these spiritual disciplines, a commitment that has reshaped my daily routines and very essence. The people around me – friends from my younger days, colleagues from various phases of my career, and even casual acquaintances – often express their intrigue and curiosity. They wonder about the catalyst for such a significant shift. What sparked this deep dive into a world so different from the one I had inhabited for so long?

My family, too, has watched this transformation with a mixture of astonishment and confusion. My parents, brothers, daughters, and wife, who have seen the various facets of my life unfold, now observe a man who is markedly different from the one they thought they knew. This new path I've taken is not just a phase but a poignant turning point that has introduced a new peace and purpose into my life.

This unexpected journey has become a topic of discussion, a point of reflection, and, for some, a source of inspiration. It invites questions, prompts discussions, and even challenges the perceptions of those who thought they knew me best. The change is not just in what I do, but consequentially in how I view and engage with the world. As I continue to explore these spiritual depths, I invite those around me to reconsider their paths and discover new ways to understand and navigate the complexities of life.

The Road Less Traveled

Sometimes, choosing a path less traveled by those around you can feel like wandering through a dense, uncharted forest. The isolation isn't just physical – it's emotional and existential. You are aware of the eyes watching you, some with curiosity, others with skepticism. They see your steps veering off the expected track, diverging from the well-trodden paths they are comfortable walking. The further you venture, the fainter their voices become until you are enveloped in a silence that amplifies your solitude.

This loneliness is palpable because it's not just about being alone. It's about feeling misunderstood and the quiet ache for someone to see not just the strangeness of your journey but more of its beauty and bravery. It's about wishing for someone to understand where you are going and why you need to go there. In this solitude, even the most supportive friends and family can seem distant, their understanding held back by the invisible restraints of their own experiences.

Yet, in the heart of this isolation, there's a significant kind of growth – a silent flowering of the self that often goes unseen. Each step forward is an act of courage, a testament to the strength of my convictions. In these moments of solitude, I find a deeper connection with myself, a clearer vision of my purpose that, one day, might bridge the gaps that once seemed impassable. It is one of the goals of this book to do just that.

Reflections on the Journey

The sheer volume of content I engage with is overwhelming. Each night, as I open up my portals, I witness hundreds of souls in motion, an experience that is surreal. These visions of angels, archangels, and other mystical entities reveal the intricate processes of spiritual movement. Moreover, this continuous exposure has led me to believe that I, myself, may be having a significant, almost celestial impact on them. Opening up a portal, allowing countless human and animal souls to transition more swiftly to their destined realms, has earned me their gratitude.

Each meditation session unfolds like a journey into a mystical landscape. When I delve into the quietude of my mind, I often ask questions about past lives. The answers come to me as vivid projections, each a crystal-clear tableau of another existence. These experiences are intensely personal and deeply moving, opening my eyes to the vast complexities of life beyond the immediate.

As I navigate this inner world, I encounter visions that reveal the secret mechanics of the universe. I witness the transition of souls, an intricate dance of energy moving from one plane to another. I see creatures from distant planets, each with unique forms and existences that challenge my understanding of life.

While personal and introspective, these insights connect me to a broader narrative. They are not just affirmations of my role, but gateways to understanding the interconnectedness of all existence. The knowledge I gain through meditation doesn't elevate my importance but deepens my appreciation for the complex tapestry of life that extends beyond our conventional perceptions.

At the heart of my quest has been the vital need to establish and nurture a connection with benevolent entities from other realms. These entities have shown me incredible love; through them, I've experienced the vastness of affection that the universe holds for each of us. One of my primary motivations has been to help others realize this, too — to understand how much you are cherished by the cosmos and how this love is there to support and uplift you.

Reflecting on the broader scope of my journey, it encompasses themes of light, love, and deep connection. It's about expanding my mystical understanding and actively seeking out those spiritual beings who freely offer their love. These connections span different lifetimes and dimensions, enriching my existence and knowledge of the universe.

If I were to simply stop today, declaring my retirement to live leisurely as many do, it wouldn't align with the essence of my purpose. There's a specific reason I've returned to Earth that compels me to leverage my resources — time, financial means, and opportunities that many lightworkers might not have. I am fortunate to have the freedom to meditate as I wish, in a chapel of my own, and to collaborate with gifted individuals like Jessica Franzini, who help articulate and share my experiences and insights.

Ultimately, if I were to distill everything down to its core, my journey, as sentimental as it might sound, is truly about love. It's about discovering love's boundless presence in the universe and finding ways to manifest that love in the world around me, assisting others in their spiritual and personal growth. This pursuit of love and connection is my path and the essence of why I am here ... to support you.

I Finished the Book. Now What?

My journey is a continuous evolution of deepening my abilities and understanding, aimed at refining my skills to directly perceive and communicate with spiritual entities without the aid of cameras or specialized filters. Currently, my interactions with these entities are mediated through images and videos. While I have become proficient in this method, my ultimate goal is to see and communicate with these entities directly in my immediate surroundings.

As I advance down this path, I constantly think about my lifelong commitment to learning and exploration. Regardless of my age, whether 85 or 90, I envision myself still engaged with videos, still examining pictures, and still immersed in reading and learning about the deeper, more mysterious aspects of mysticism and the occult. Assisted by my mystic guide, Tula, I delve deeper into understanding and connecting with the unseen, enhancing my perception and interaction with the spiritual realms.

The progression of my journey involves a significant focus on interpreting and creating a language from the symbols communicated by the souls who visit me. These symbols, often aligning with Hebrew script, convey philosophical messages, such as interpretations of cosmic events like the eclipse of April 8th, 2024. There is no denying the scientific astronomical explanation for why an eclipse occurs. However, on the spiritual side, the messages I received that day were that the eclipse was an opportunity to "view God."

The energy required to facilitate these nighttime video sessions is considerable. The souls manage and manipulate this energy with remarkable efficiency, using the lights in their realm and the natural energy grids that connect our universes. Despite the possibility that my capacity to receive visions as vividly as before might diminish due to the extensive energy involved, I am driven to improve this communication, inspired by the transformative impact of past visions that have been incredibly meaningful to me.

Another goal is to deepen my connection with the Holy Ones and my spirit guides to a level where I can clearly see and communicate with them daily. My assistant, Dominique, has experienced a transformation that has been significantly influenced by his own spiritual journey, exemplifying the absolute impact these connections can have. Observing his progress has been incredibly inspiring, and it motivates me to facilitate similar transformations for more people, helping them experience the power and positivity of aligning with the spiritual path, ultimately changing their lives for the better.

I want to explore the spiritual realm further, perhaps even experiencing it more directly in dreams, where the boundary between our physical world and the spiritual plane thins. This exploration would deepen my understanding of my spirit guides and open pathways for others to access these compelling realms of love and guidance.

Ultimately, my goal is to advance significantly on my spiritual journey, potentially ascending to higher spiritual realms and higher mansion worlds. These realms, inhabited by beings who have evolved beyond ordinary material existence, offer opportunities to explore even more elevated experiences and gain insights that mark heightened spiritual development.

This journey is about creating a ripple effect of spiritual awakening and growth that can touch the lives of many, fostering a community of enlightened individuals who support and uplift each other. Through technology and education, I plan to host various events to promote learning, spiritual growth, and community action, propelling us towards enriching more lives and significantly impacting the world.

My path is intricately woven with guidance and insight from my spiritual mentors, who illuminate the way forward with a wisdom that transcends the ordinary. This journey is far from random. It is a meticulously charted course through the spiritual landscape, where every step is imbued with intention and purpose. My mentors, both seen and unseen, serve as navigators, pointing me toward the lessons I need to absorb, the symbols I need to decipher, and the experiences I must undergo to deepen my understanding and spiritual growth.

These guides are custodians of ancient knowledge and mystical truths entrusted with the responsibility of passing on these sacred teachings. They help me discern the significance of various symbols that appear in my life. These symbols often carry messages from the spiritual realm encoded in a language that transcends words. These symbols might manifest in everyday occurrences or moments of deep meditation, each a puzzle piece in the grand mosaic of my spiritual awakening.

Encounters, too, are arranged with precision on this journey. These meetings are never coincidental, whether with people who bring important lessons or with spiritual entities that offer cogent insights. They are orchestrated to push me towards greater self-awareness and enlightenment, challenging me to evolve and embrace a broader perspective of the universe.

My mentors also carefully select experiences along this path, designed to test and expand my spiritual boundaries. These experiences could be challenges that force me to confront my inner fears and doubts or moments of sublime beauty that remind me of the divine connection that threads through all existence. Each experience is a stepping stone, a moment of transformation that propels me further along this sacred path.

This guided exploration is a dynamic interplay between the known and the unknown, the seen and the unseen. My mentors ensure that each step I take leads to greater wisdom and spiritual fulfillment. As I continue on this path, I am constantly reminded that this journey is not just about reaching a destination but about the transformation that occurs within me as I travel, guided by those who have walked this way before and who know its intricate turns and hidden passages.

Egypt Is Calling

Soon I will be embarking on an enriching journey to Egypt, a land steeped in ancient wisdom and spiritual resonance, particularly connected to my past life experiences centered around the mystical Philae temple. Accompanied by my assistant Dominique and Ryan, my documentarian, we plan to capture the essence of Egypt's rich historical and spiritual landscape. This endeavor is not just about filming; it's an exploratory mission that might also spark the inspiration for another book, depending on how our current projects unfold.

Our itinerary is deeply intertwined with my quest to understand past lives and delving into the Akashic Records, described below. Egypt offers a unique backdrop to investigate the enigmatic symbols that frequently surface in my videos. These symbols hint at profound spiritual contracts and pathways. These symbols often evoke themes related to ancient covenants and mystical journeys, suggesting that specific "doors" of knowledge are waiting to be opened.

Moreover, this trip presents a significant opportunity for teaching and sharing insights. Egypt's ancient landscapes provide the perfect setting for engaging with fellow seekers and enthusiasts, allowing me to conduct sessions or informal discussions contributing to our collective spiritual enlightenment. This aligns seamlessly with my ongoing commitment to my own spiritual growth — a journey continually nurtured by the guidance and wisdom of my spiritual mentors.

Through this blend of filming, research, and engagement, the trip to Egypt is set to be a multifaceted expedition. It is poised to enrich my understanding and offer new perspectives that will contribute to my spiritual journey and my professional endeavors in literature and documentary filmmaking.

Akashic Records

The Akashic Records are believed to be a cosmic library containing detailed records of every thought, word, and deed of every living being across all times — past, present, and future. This repository encompasses all life forms and entities, maintaining a nonjudgmental record of each soul's journey through infinity.

The concept of the Akashic Records was popularized in modern times by Helena Blavatsky, the founder of the Theosophical movement in the late 19th century. Blavatsky, influenced by Eastern philosophies and the idea of a universal truth, claimed to have learned about the records from Tibetan monks. These records, she said, existed in the "akasha," or ether, which is considered a fundamental element of reality in Eastern traditions and is closely linked to the concept of karma.

The concept of Akasha as linked to karma involves the idea that every action, thought, and consequence is recorded in this cosmic substance, thus forming the foundation for the cycle of karma. In Eastern philosophical and spiritual traditions, karma is not merely a system of punishments and rewards, but a law of moral causation, an integral principle of the universe. Here's how Akasha and karma are intertwined:

1. **Recording of Actions and Consequences:** The Akashic Records are not just historical accounts but also contain the emotional and spiritual implications of each event. Therefore, every individual's actions are imprinted in the Akasha, contributing to their karmic legacy.
2. **Influence on Personal and Universal Karma:** The Akashic Records can be thought of as a cosmic database that influences both individual destinies and broader cosmic patterns. Each action an individual takes impacts their future, not only through direct consequences but also through the Akashic imprints, which can shape the conditions and circumstances they encounter. This view supports the belief that past lives and reincarnation are influenced by one's previous actions as recorded in the Akasha.

3. **Spiritual Insights and Growth:** In several traditions, accessing the Akashic Records is possible through deep meditation or psychic abilities. Mystics, yogis, and spiritual practitioners who claim to access these records often describe receiving insights that help in personal growth and understanding the nature of karma. They suggest that by understanding one's Akashic record, an individual can work towards resolving past karmic debts and fostering spiritual advancement.
4. **Guiding Ethical Behavior:** The permanence of the Akashic Records acts as a moral compass for many adherents. Knowing that every act is recorded in the Akasha encourages ethical behavior, fostering a sense of responsibility and accountability. This concept underscores the karmic principle that every action has consequences, thus promoting a more conscientious approach to life.

Akasha's linkage to karma is central in depicting how individual actions perpetuate through time, influencing both the course of one's life and the broader cosmic order. This interconnection underscores a holistic view of the universe where individual deeds contribute to an ongoing cosmic narrative.

Blavatsky used her psychic abilities and astral projection to access these records, gaining a substantial following. Similarly, metaphysician Rudolf Steiner and contemporary physicist Ervin Laszlo have also referenced the Akashic Records, suggesting that every human action leaves a trace in these etheric realms, and these traces influence human ideals like harmony and equanimity.

The Akashic Records are sometimes likened to the "Book of Life" mentioned in the Bible, where a heavenly record of every life supposedly exists. Prominent psychic Edgar Cayce, known for his detailed readings from the Akashic Records, described it as a nonphysical plane that chronicles all souls' past, present, and future.

Accessing the Akashic Records has become popular, with numerous methods described in books, blogs, and videos, each tailored to individual experiences and preferences. People report various experiences when accessing the records, from seeing guides and past life "movies" to receiving auditory messages. While some succeed on their first attempt, others may need persistent effort over time.

For those interested in exploring this fascinating concept, studying the works and teachings of Edgar Cayce, Helena Blavatsky, and Ervin Laszlo provides a solid foundation. The Akashic Records offer profound insights into the soul's history and potential future paths, making them an invaluable resource for anyone curious about the deeper aspects of their existence.

Retreat of My Dreams

I am developing a unique wellness resort that blends tranquility with spiritual growth, set in the serene surroundings of Louisville, Kentucky – a city currently lacking such facilities. This sanctuary will offer a unique spa experience characterized by the soothing sounds of a church bell that rings throughout the property. This blend of the spiritual with the serene will enhance the tranquil atmosphere of the resort. This spa will serve as a cornerstone of the resort's appeal, providing a space for reflection and rejuvenation.

As we explore the property's potential, the enchanting beauty of the house overlooking the lake becomes apparent. This setting is breathtaking and functional, offering a perfect retreat from everyday life and a gathering space for minds and souls to engage and grow. The resort is designed to accommodate about 30 to 45 couples, creating an intimate environment that fosters closeness and personal interaction.

The resort's design includes clear, flowing waters and meditation trails that will lead guests to mystical spots on the property, designed to evoke the legendary allure of places like Glastonbury Tor in the United Kingdom. Inspired by energy vortex experiences similar to those in Sedona, I plan to integrate elements that enhance the natural landscape with expansive water features and vortex-inspired experiences, providing a transformative experience that resonates with our guests' spiritual and aesthetic inclinations.

Additionally, the resort will feature selective classes to foster a community of learners engaged in meditation and inquiry, facilitating a shared journey of spiritual growth. All of the planned features cater to a growing trend in wellness tourism, where guests seek to unwind and connect with their higher selves.

This sanctuary will also serve as a portal for peace and passage. It will focus particularly on animal welfare, reflecting my commitment to environmental stewardship. This space will cater to human guests and also provide a haven for animals, integrating my spiritual pursuits with practical actions to foster a harmonious coexistence.

Envisioned as a place of peace and reflection, the resort aims to be a spiritual haven that subtly encourages guests to explore their deeper selves without feeling overwhelmed by overt spiritual motifs. This concept is driven by a genuine demand I observe daily, where individuals are eager for new beginnings and meaningful experiences. Through this project, I want to meet this demand and create an unparalleled retreat that enriches spiritual lives and provides a peaceful respite for those looking to escape their hectic routines.

The story of this land further enriches its potential. Initially purchased by Imogene and Jerry Phelps, the previous owners dreamed of constructing a turn-of-the-century village. Jerry, an anesthesiologist, ambitiously built a general store and relocated seven historic cabins from various parts of Kentucky to this land. They meticulously restored these cabins and even cleared land to build two miles of roads. Jerry filled the general store with period-appropriate items and created a space that breathes history.

However, despite his efforts and vision, Jerry faced challenges in attracting people to this beautiful retreat and, unfortunately, after developing Parkinson's, decided to sell the property, which I then acquired. Today, the property boasts magical views of the surrounding hills and lake, making it a picturesque location that is simply captivating. The historical cabins, some of which date back to the turn of the century, add depth and authenticity to the experience. The original residents' tombstones have been preserved near the cabins, providing guests with a tangible connection to the past inhabitants of this property.

My Legacy

As I contemplate the legacy I hope to leave behind, my thoughts often converge on two central aspirations. Firstly, I wish for my life to be remembered as one that significantly impacted many, deeply enriching their lives both spiritually and personally. My vision extends beyond simply aiding people through challenging times; I aim to foster enlightenment, improve karma, and enhance overall well-being, helping individuals feel more complete and at peace.

I envision a future where, upon my passing, my contributions are celebrated by a community that I've touched. I imagine my funeral will be attended by many who would speak of the personal connections we shared and the impactful, positive changes I catalyzed during my time on Earth. They would recount my philanthropic efforts, highlighting how these initiatives brought about tangible improvements in the lives of others, not just through financial support but through empowering and uplifting communities.

Beyond my public and charitable endeavors, I value my roles as a devoted father and a loving husband even more so. These personal relationships are fundamental to me, embodying my core values and representing what I consider most meaningful in life. I hope these roles are remembered as vividly as my professional and philanthropic efforts, reflecting a life well-lived that prioritized genuine connections, kindness, and altruism over material wealth or status.

Looking forward, I see myself cherishing not only the deep personal connections I've nurtured as a husband, father, and grandfather, but the positive environment I've strived to create for my employees. These relationships and contributions are integral parts of my legacy, emphasizing the breadth of my impact. Friends in my meditation circle describe me as an old soul with a powerful past, and I feel a strong sense of responsibility to fulfill this potential — a mission that seems entrusted to me.

Ultimately, my journey is about contributing to the spiritual progression of others while advancing through spiritual echelons myself. I am committed to exploring new realms and deepening connections with spiritual guides instrumental in my development. This dual focus on outreach and personal evolution defines my path and the profound legacy I work to create — a legacy of enriching lives and fostering spiritual awakening.

Love Is the Currency of the Universe

Love is the currency of the universe is a powerful and transformative concept. It suggests that love, not material wealth or power, is the accurate measure of value and exchange. This notion challenges the traditional paradigms of success and influence, proposing that the interactions and transactions that truly matter are those conducted with love.

When we consider love a currency, we imagine a world where every act of kindness, every gesture of compassion, and every moment of understanding contributes to a wealth that benefits all of humanity. This is not a currency that can be hoarded, or that diminishes with use; instead, it multiplies and spreads, enriching the lives of the giver and the receiver alike.

Practically, making love the currency I work with here on Earth means redefining my actions and interactions. It involves assessing the impact of my behaviors not just on my immediate surroundings but on the broader community and the world at large. Every decision, from the simplest acts of daily life to major life choices, is guided by the evaluative question: "Is this spreading love?"

This approach requires a shift from a mindset of scarcity, where resources like money and power are tightly controlled and competed over, to one of abundance, where there is always enough love to go around and to spare. It fosters environments where collaboration and generosity replace competition and greed.

Moreover, treating love as a currency means recognizing and appreciating each person's intrinsic value. It encourages looking beyond external differences and finding the common thread of humanity that connects us all. This viewpoint helps dissolve barriers and build bridges, fostering a more inclusive and empathetic society.

On a larger scale, adopting love as a currency can drive profound societal and global changes. It can lead to more equitable economic systems, compassionate governance, and cooperative international relations. Communities and nations prioritizing love and compassion tend to be more resilient, happier, and more successful in creating sustainable and peaceful environments.

Ultimately, by operating with love as my currency, I commit to a life that continuously seeks to contribute positively, promote well-being, and uplift spirits. It's about creating a legacy not measured by material accumulation but by the amount of love shared and the lives touched. This commitment aligns with the belief that the richest life is one spent investing in the well-being of others, creating a ripple effect that can transform the world.

The Beginning

This current chapter of my life is indelibly marked by themes of growth, learning, and sharing. These themes are intricately woven into my daily existence and highlighted by the celestial companions who illuminate my path. These spiritual guides, whether perceived as ethereal entities or manifestations of my deeper consciousness, serve as beacons, casting light on the darker corners of my understanding and offering clarity in moments of uncertainty.

Each day unfolds as a new page in this ongoing journey, where every experience adds a layer to my soul's evolution. Whether engaging with new ideas, confronting challenging situations, or reveling in moments of joy, each circumstance is imbued with the potential for personal and spiritual growth. The symbols that emerge in my life often appearing as synchronicities or serendipitous events act as signposts. They guide my decisions and infuse my path with meaning, suggesting that nothing occurs by chance but as part of a larger, divine tapestry.

The connections I forge with others play a pivotal role in this journey. Each interaction – whether fleeting or long-standing – is an exchange of energy that has the potential to uplift, heal, and transform. By sharing my insights and experiences, I not only contribute to the growth of others but also deepen my own understanding and spiritual practice. This reciprocity is a cornerstone of my life's work, underscoring the importance of community and mutual support in the quest for enlightenment.

As I progress, I am increasingly aware of how these elements – experience, symbol, and connection – intertwine to propel me forward. This propulsion is about moving through life and rising to higher planes of awareness where the spiritual becomes more tangible, and the mundane aspects of daily life gain meaningful significance.

This extraordinary journey of enlightenment and service is not a solitary trek but a shared voyage. It invites a continual exchange of wisdom and compassion with like-minded souls, thus extending far beyond my immediate surroundings. It is a path marked by discovering inner truths and sharing these revelations with the world, ensuring that this chapter of my life contributes to a legacy of spiritual awakening and collective elevation.

Chapter 11

How to Start Your Journey

> *It does not matter how slowly you go as long as you do not stop.*
>
> *Confucius*

In presenting my experiences, knowledge, thoughts, and insights, it is my sincerest hope that my book serves as a catalyst for you to set forth on your own spiritual journey. My goal is to inspire, offer guidance, and provide resources and support for you to venture into the unknown.

The act of choosing to read *Behind the Veil* was likely not arbitrary. It's conceivable that there was an underlying motivation or a whisper of intuition urging you to select this particular book from the various options available. Perhaps a compelling force or a serendipitous reason guided your decision to engage with this material.

By delving into the pages of this book, you are either initiating a new journey or continuing an existing one. This reading is a step in your personal evolution. It is not just an act of consumption but a meaningful engagement that aligns with your path.

One of the most significant challenges individuals face with personal development and spiritual growth is the demanding nature of daily life. Particularly for younger people, life's complexities and hustle and bustle can seem like formidable barriers to significant spiritual development. Observations from places like the Earth and Spirit Center reveal that those who often engage in meditation classes are predominantly older women, many of whom are retired and have the time to commit to such practices. This demographic trend highlights a broader truth about life's stages and time allocation for spiritual growth.

As I mentioned in Chapter 9, however, a journey toward spiritual enlightenment doesn't necessitate an extreme transformation or withdrawal from society. Indeed, your spiritual path will not always be straightforward or free from time constraints. Still, you don't need to emulate Buddha or retreat to a monastery to make significant spiritual progress. Instead, remember that I and others who have walked this path advocate for cultivating an inner sanctuary. This personal spiritual practice benefits the individual, and positively influences their surroundings and loved ones. This internal spiritual church becomes a source of light and guidance, enriching one's life and the lives of those around them, demonstrating that spiritual growth and everyday life can coexist harmoniously.

You should understand that while pursuing this path may require balancing numerous aspects of daily life, the journey is supported by a host of spiritual entities eager to assist. These guides are infinitely patient, understanding that our time on Earth is brief in the soul's eternal voyage. Beyond our earthly existence, an array of adventures awaits across various realms and planets, offering endless opportunities for growth and exploration in our soul's evolution.

As mentioned earlier, author Diana Cooper writes in great detail about angels' and archangels' roles as universal symbols of hope, guidance, and purity. As you delve into your spiritual journey, the stories and teachings of angels and archangels can provide strength and guidance. These beings are portrayed as accessible guides offering wisdom and support. Their diverse roles across cultures, as protectors, negotiators, or sources of enlightenment, highlight their significance in providing a multifaceted support system for individuals seeking spiritual growth.

The detailed accounts of archangels, each with specific attributes and roles, invite you to explore how these celestial guides can offer targeted support and insight. For example, invoking Archangel Michael for protection or Raphael for healing can personalize your spiritual practice, allowing for a deeper connection with these powerful entities.

I encourage you to engage with these beings, integrating their high vibrations and pure energies into your life through meditation, prayer, and other spiritual practices. Such engagement is a step toward personal and collective empowerment, aligning you with the divine and enhancing your journey toward spiritual enlightenment.

In her book, *Birthing a New Civilization: Transition to the New Golden Age in 2032*, Cooper describes the divine vision for our planet as one where love and compassion prevail, transcending individual egos and the myriad distractions that often preoccupy us. This aspiration isn't just wishful thinking; it's a goal with a sense of urgency, with significant transformations hoped for by 2032. This timeline sets a compelling backdrop for anyone engaging with my book.

The Role of Nature

You begin to witness significant transformations when you steadfastly engage in your spiritual practices, be it through dedicated reading, meditation, or other forms of spiritual work. Your cognitive functions become sharper, your mindfulness deepens, and your meditation experiences grow increasingly profound. These changes collectively foster an enhancement in the quality of your life, a phenomenon confirmed by the personal experiences of many.

In your journey of self-exploration and spiritual growth, reconnecting with nature is pivotal. As you step away from the urban environments of concrete and steel to immerse yourself in the natural world, you experience a profound sense of grounding and connection, something deeply craved yet often elusive in contemporary life. Engaging directly with the earth, feeling its texture underfoot, and surrounding yourself with the living tapestry of nature is an inherently human experience that has become a rarity in the modern world. Your daily life, predominantly spent within the confines of constructed spaces, typically leads to a disconnection from the natural world, with significant implications for your well-being.

In its purest form, nature possesses an unmatched capacity to heal and rejuvenate, offering a holistic form of healing that encompasses your physical, emotional, and spiritual dimensions. Grounding yourself in nature, whether walking barefoot, spending time amidst trees, or simply being present in a natural setting, is an act of reconnection to your fundamental essence that gets overshadowed by urban existence. This reconnection is symbolic and involves a direct, physical interaction that can benefit your health. The natural charge of the earth's surface can neutralize stress, reduce inflammation, and promote physical well-being.

Thus, grounding in nature transcends being a mere respite from your daily routines; it is an essential re-engagement with a primal source of energy and healing. As you seek to cultivate a healthier, more balanced life, embracing this intrinsic connection to the natural world presents a pathway toward enhanced physical health and a deeper sense of inner peace and connectedness. This reconnection with nature is integral to a holistic approach to living, offering real benefits that can resonate through all facets of your existence.

Dirt Church

Recently, I experienced a massage from a practitioner well-versed in trigger point therapy. This session was much more than just physical relief for my troublesome neck. An avid dirt biker, the therapist shared insights that resonated deeply with me, particularly about his unique way of connecting spiritually. He and his fellow riders refer to their Sunday morning races in open, natural spaces as attending "dirt church." This term struck a chord with me, encapsulating their meaningful bond with nature, the thrill of the ride, and the camaraderie among riders, all of which they perceive as their form of spiritual practice.

This "dirt church" concept beautifully illustrates the diverse ways individuals can find spiritual connection and meaning in their lives beyond traditional settings or practices. It's a reminder that spirituality can be as varied and personal as the individuals seeking it, whether in the quietness of a physical church, the exhilarating freedom of racing through nature, or the simple daily interactions we have with the world.

This notion aligns with what I believe is a core message from divine teachings: the call to connect with the earth, our fellow beings, and the broader community. It's a testament to the idea that every person, regardless of their background or beliefs, has the potential to experience profound spiritual connections in their own unique way.

Should We Ask, "What Would Jesus Do?"

Navigating the landscape of spirituality doesn't necessarily require outward symbols like "What Would Jesus Do" bracelets. While these items can be meaningful for some, spiritual connection transcends such physical manifestations. The conversation about spirituality often intertwines with references to religious texts like the Bible, which holds significant truth and value for me. However, I'm aware of a growing sentiment where people feel overwhelmed or jaded by constant references to scripture in mainstream discourse.

Living a spiritual life and forging a connection with the divine doesn't have to be anchored strictly in religious practices or symbols. It's more about the individual's journey and the authenticity of their experience. For those curious about exploring spirituality, particularly connecting with the "other side" or reaching a higher self, there's a rich array of modalities to explore beyond traditional frameworks.

Moreover, discussing life beyond this physical realm, particularly the concept of learning in "mansion worlds," prompts a vital question: What is there to learn? This question opens up a fascinating dialogue about the continuous nature of spiritual and personal growth, suggesting that our journey of understanding and connection doesn't end with this earthly existence but continues in various forms and dimensions.

Ultimately, the journey to spiritual enlightenment is intimately personal and can be enriched by many practices and beliefs. It's about finding what strikes a chord with you, what helps you connect to a greater sense of purpose and understanding, and how to integrate these insights into your everyday life to foster a deeper sense of connection and fulfillment.

The Importance of Discernment

Before you close this book, it is imperative to discuss the idea and significance of discernment, particularly in the interplay between intuition and discernment in decision-making. Intuition can be seen as an instinctive feeling that often relies on past experiences to guide us. For example, suppose a past negative experience with a drummer has influenced you. In that case, meeting another drummer might trigger an intuitive caution. However, discernment is critical in differentiating between this intuitive reaction and guidance from more profound, spiritual sources that encourage us to view situations without past biases, potentially leading to beneficial outcomes.

Developing the ability to discern between these different sources of guidance is akin to the serendipity of stumbling upon a new meditation center when all you were seeking was a quiet place for reflection. Such moments of synchronicity can be the starting points for a deeper exploration into how the universe communicates with us, providing signs and guiding us toward greater self-awareness and growth.

Discernment is not just critical for spiritual growth. It is essential in navigating the various forms of guidance we receive, whether from our inner selves or spiritual entities offering wisdom. This skill enables us to sift through and interpret the subtle signals we encounter, like intuitive nudges or synchronicities, while being aware of our biases and previous experiences. It's about developing the ability to distinguish between personal intuition shaped by past events and the insights provided by universal or divine wisdom, guiding our actions and decisions toward a path of greater self-awareness and spiritual development.

To me, discernment is foundational to the spiritual journey, acting as the crucial pivot point for all spiritual endeavors. Its value is immeasurable, yet it is equally challenging to master. Discernment involves processing and understanding the guidance you receive, whether through spiritual advisors, during moments of prayer, or through personal meditative practices. It's about recognizing the authenticity of the messages you receive, distinguishing between divine guidance and the plethora of thoughts that flood your mind daily.

Where to Get Information

Engaging with spiritual content through books has long been fundamental to my personal growth and learning. Over the years, I've come to value the depth and authenticity that books offer, especially when contrasted with the Internet's vast, often overwhelming nature. However, as with any source of information, not every book I pick up resonates with my inner spirit. Sometimes, I encounter texts that feel disconnected from my spiritual path, signaling a misalignment with my beliefs or current spiritual journey. Recognizing this alignment or misalignment is an essential exercise in discernment. This skill is crucial in selecting the suitable spiritual materials that enrich and support one's development.

At the age of 65, I find myself increasingly skeptical of the Internet as a primary source for deep, meaningful spiritual exploration. One of the challenges with initiating a spiritual inquiry through a search engine is how it propels you to choose divergent paths. Not all these paths are constructive or relevant to the genuine quest for spiritual enlightenment. Search algorithms, while designed to streamline and guide our exploration, can occasionally mislead us into disparate or potentially misleading territories of information. This digital labyrinth can distract and confuse rather than enlighten.

In contrast, reading a book provides a more structured and immersive experience. Books allow for a deep dive into subjects without the constant interruptions of pop-ups or hyperlinks that might divert your attention. In my experience guiding others on their spiritual paths, I've observed many getting sidetracked by various online resources. These distractions range from the intricacies of quantum physics theories to the wild realms of alien conspiracies. Such diversions dilute their initial focus, which might have been centered on understanding the principles of Buddhism or the teachings about archangels.

The nature of the Internet, with its endless array of interpretations and viewpoints, poses a significant challenge in maintaining a focused and coherent path in one's spiritual exploration. On the other hand, a well-researched and thoughtfully composed book generally offers a more consolidated and reliable source of knowledge. The author's insights are typically well-considered and presented in a manner that fosters understanding and reflection, free from the erratic shifts in topic and quality often found online.

Discernment is thus indispensable, whether delving into books or navigating digital content. It involves distinguishing between what genuinely aids spiritual advancement and what merely detracts or distracts. This skill helps filter the noise and focus on the essence of spiritual learning.

The thoughtful selection of spiritual books over indiscriminate Internet browsing can significantly enhance one's journey toward spiritual enlightenment. Books provide a focused, in-depth approach to learning that needs to be included in the fragmented, hyperlinked environment of online resources. As we seek to deepen our understanding and connection with the spiritual realm, the clarity, depth, and focus offered by books become beneficial and essential.

How to Begin

Let's explore the intriguing process of initiating your spiritual journey. This is a subject particularly captivating, as I've dedicated time to assisting others in beginning their own spiritual quests. The foundational step is the clear decision to embark on this path. It's about consciously committing and allocating time to cultivate a practice. This practice, essentially a personal ritual, can occur at any moment, day or night, and involves turning inward to engage in meditation or mindfulness with consistent dedication. The aim here is to evolve from being a seeker to becoming a discoverer of spiritual realms, encounters, and entities.

As discussed earlier, my enthusiasm in this realm led me to explore connections with my spirit guides. My favorite book, *Ask Your Guides* by Sonia Choquette, is among the many resources available. I often recommend it.

Initiating communication with your guides begins with simple meditation and a methodical connecting process. First, you inquire about their names and roles. There are predominantly four types of guides to get acquainted with:

your teacher guide, your joy and pleasure guide, your guardian or protector, and your health guide. These guides are pivotal in navigating your life and spiritual growth. As you continue along this path, you will meet many more, as I have.

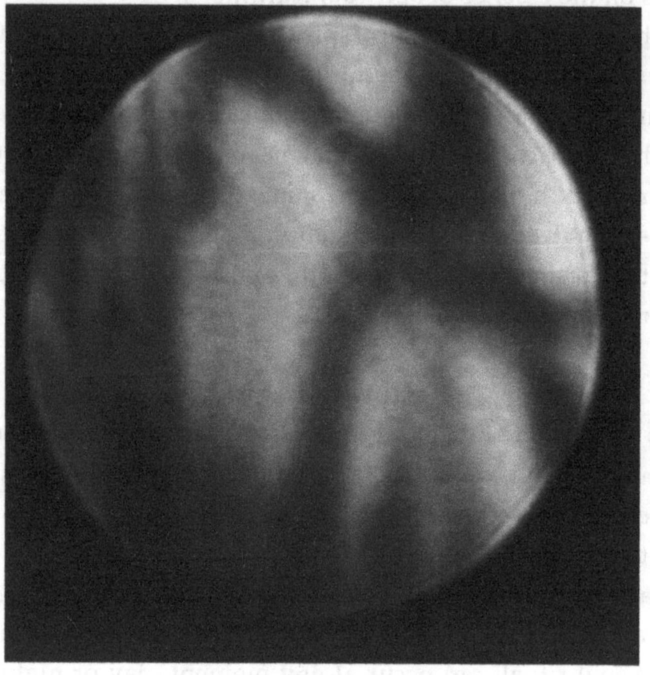

Angel holding a lantern in place.

Beyond meditation, using a pendulum can be an effective method to enhance communication with your guides. By asking it to confirm your name or respond to simple yes/no questions, you can develop trust in the responses, interpreting the pendulum's movements as communication from your guides.

In addition to these practices, I find profound value in reading. The books I select are not random; they align with my path, almost as if they've been placed in my orbit for a reason. Through reading, I receive confirmations and insights, reinforcing the guidance I receive from my spiritual journey.

Embarking on this journey is a multifaceted process, intertwining practices like meditation, pendulum use, and reading to deepen your understanding and connection with the spiritual realm. This journey is about engaging, learning, and evolving with the guidance and support of unseen but profoundly present spiritual entities.

I advocate for joining meditation groups or finding a spiritual community where you can learn and grow with others on a similar path. Another vital step in advancing your spiritual journey is finding a mentor. This can be challenging, but your spiritual development can accelerate significantly once you connect with the right mentor. You might encounter potential mentors in various settings, from bookstores to spiritual workshops, often based on recommendations from like-minded individuals.

The journey to deepen your spiritual understanding is nuanced, where discernment plays a key role in navigating the vast sea of information becoming available.

Spiritual skills are not exclusive to a select few; they are accessible to everyone willing to invest the time and effort. The range of spiritual practices is vast, encompassing various modalities, from yoga and Reiki to more unique practices like breathwork, which utilizes the power of breathing to achieve mental clarity and spiritual connection.

If you are searching for more than what your current life has to offer, and if you yearn to be astonished by a spiritually transformative event, understanding these concepts is crucial. Such events can be as profound as a vision, a vivid dream, a miraculous occurrence, or a moment of undeniable spiritual connection that invigorates the body and soul, igniting a desire for further exploration and understanding.

Every person has the potential to develop their spiritual abilities. It requires patience, commitment, and a willingness to delve into the unknown. This journey emphasizes personal growth and ethical living, aligning with spiritual teachings that advocate for love, simplicity, and integrity. By following these principles and dedicating oneself to exploring spirituality, every individual can unfold their spiritual potential, encounter their guides, and experience the innate beauty of the spiritual realm.

My aspiration is to serve as a channel for this universal spirituality, steering clear of doctrinal debates. My expertise lies in something other than theological scholarship, and I have no intention of diving into religious disputes. Instead, I find beauty in the accessibility of spiritual connection. It's not about academic accolades or scriptural mastery; it's about the heart's capacity to reach out and touch the divine.

In a world where credentials often take center stage, I emphasize that a deep, meaningful spiritual life doesn't require formal education or a thorough grounding in religious texts. It's about the personal journey, the individual search for meaning, and the unique ways we each connect with something greater than ourselves. By embracing this broader understanding of spirituality, we can make strides toward a world that's more empathetic, connected, and spiritually enriched.

Daily Practices

The following are clear action steps that you can incorporate into your daily or weekly schedule:

1. **Meditation:** Establish a daily meditation practice, starting with a few minutes each day and gradually increasing the duration. Meditation can help quiet the mind, connect with inner wisdom, and open your mind to spiritual guidance.
2. **Journaling:** Maintain a spiritual journal where you can reflect on your experiences, emotions, and the insights you receive during meditation or at other moments of introspection.

3. **Engage with Nature:** Spend time in nature regularly, as this can help you feel connected to the earth and the universe, fostering a sense of oneness and spiritual awareness.
4. **Read and Reflect:** Explore other spiritual texts and teachings, reflecting on how these align with your experiences and the insights gained from this book.
5. **Practice Mindfulness:** Living in the present moment is crucial for spiritual growth.
6. **Connect with Community:** Seek out like-minded individuals and spiritual communities. Sharing experiences and insights can enhance your spiritual journey and provide support and encouragement.
7. **Attend Workshops or Retreats:** Try to attend spiritual workshops or retreats, which can offer intensive opportunities for growth, learning, and connection.
8. **Invoke Angelic Guidance:** Call your angels and archangels for guidance, protection, and inspiration.
9. **Practice Gratitude:** I encourage you to begin a daily practice of gratitude, which can shift your perspective, open your heart, and attract positive energy and experiences.
10. **Explore Creative Expression:** Explore your spirituality through creative outlets like art, music, or dance, which can be powerful mediums for expressing and exploring one's inner world.
11. **Develop Your Intuition:** Work on honing your intuition. Pay attention to your gut feelings and interpret synchronicities.
12. **Perform Acts of Kindness:** Regular acts of kindness and compassion can elevate your own energy and contribute positively to the world around you.
13. **Seek Silence:** Spend time in silence daily, as silence can be a genuine teacher and conduit for spiritual insights.

14. **Set Intentions:** Set clear, positive intentions for your daily life. "Thoughts become things," Rhonda Byrne reminds us.

A Closer Look at Gratitude

Dr. Leo Buscaglia was a professor, motivational speaker, and author widely known for his dynamic lectures and writings on love, human relationships, and education. He emphasized the importance of gratitude in fostering a fulfilling and enriching life. His perspectives on gratitude are interwoven with his broader philosophical views on love and human connection, illustrating how gratitude acts as an emotion and a foundational aspect of living fully and loving others.

According to Buscaglia, gratitude is crucial in the cycle of love and positive energy exchange between individuals. He believed that appreciating the simple joys and the people in one's life can lead to a greater openness to love and be loved. Gratitude, in his view, is not a passive acknowledgement but an active celebration of life. It compels individuals to recognize the beauty in the mundane, the extraordinary in the ordinary, and the contributions of others to our well-being and happiness.

In his writings and lectures, Buscaglia encouraged people to express gratitude openly and frequently, asserting that such expressions can dramatically strengthen bonds between people. He often noted that showing appreciation can make others feel valued and loved, creating a positive feedback loop that enhances the emotional well-being of all involved. For Buscaglia, gratitude was a gateway through which individuals could acknowledge the goodness in their lives and foster an environment where positive relationships could flourish.

Moreover, Buscaglia highlighted the transformative power of gratitude in overcoming negativity and adversity. By focusing on what one has rather than what one lacks, individuals can cultivate a mindset that is more content and more resilient in the face of challenges. Gratitude, thus, serves as a buffer against bitterness and despair, enabling individuals to approach life's inevitable difficulties with a balanced perspective and a hopeful heart.

Overall, Leo Buscaglia's message about gratitude enriches the giver just as much as the receiver. It is an essential ingredient in his recipe for a loving, joyful life. Through gratitude, we improve our lives and contribute to a better, more loving world.

Protecting Your Sense of Gratitude

In her article for the March 20th issue of *Folio Weekly*, Briana Pereira discusses the phenomenon of "FOMO" (fear of missing out) and how it can diminish one's sense of gratitude. According to Pereira, FOMO is the anxiety that an exciting or interesting event may happen elsewhere, often triggered by social media posts. This feeling, she explains, is rooted in the fear of not measuring up to others, which is intensified by constant exposure to the curated, seemingly perfect lives of others on social media platforms.

Pereira emphasizes that FOMO and its social comparison can significantly undermine an individual's ability to appreciate their own life and achievements. The social comparison theory, which suggests that people determine their own social and personal worth by comparing themselves to others, plays a central role in this process. As individuals see highly idealized glimpses of others' lives online, they often feel inadequate or left behind, resulting in a decreased sense of gratitude for their own circumstances.

To combat these adverse effects, Pereira suggests several strategies. Reducing social media consumption can help lessen the exposure to unrealistic portrayals of life that feed feelings of inadequacy and FOMO. She shares anecdotes about friends who deleted their social media accounts to escape the relentless comparison and found their mental well-being improved.

Additionally, Pereira advocates for engaging in mindfulness practices and cultivating gratitude to counteract the impacts of FOMO. Practices like meditation, deep breathing exercises, and maintaining a gratitude journal can help individuals focus on the present and appreciate what they have rather than pining for what they perceive they lack. These practices foster a grounded perspective, helping to restore a sense of gratitude and satisfaction with one's life.

Pereira also advises setting realistic expectations for social engagement and seeking meaningful connections rather than striving to keep up with every social opportunity. Individuals can build more fulfilling relationships that enhance their gratitude and happiness by prioritizing quality interactions over quantity.

By understanding and addressing the underlying causes of FOMO, individuals can enhance their well-being and develop a more resilient and thankful outlook.

Personal Reflection

Reflecting on my journey, I've realized a pivotal truth: the path of spiritual growth reveals itself as you traverse it, inviting you to explore infinite possibilities. This exploration is guided not just by your conscious decisions but by the subtle nudges of your soul, heart, and spiritual guides, leading you to the depth of understanding and engagement that resonates most with your essence in spirituality and mysticism.

When I began capturing videos that unexpectedly offered spiritual insights, my initial reaction was a blend of curiosity and skepticism. I questioned whether these insights were merely serendipitous or essential milestones on my journey. Over time, it became clear that these visual revelations were not coincidental; they were vital to my growth, aligning me more closely with my intentions and life's broader path.

I've been reflecting on the significance of recent events and their alignment with my purpose of benefiting myself, others, and the universe. One remarkable incident occurred several weeks ago when I went out to take a video. Upon reviewing it the next day, I noticed that it captured my face as it is now, complete with my current hairstyle. This realization affirmed that when I request it, my image can appear in these videos.

Since then, my spiritual guide, Tula, who is more than a typical spirit guide, has become more prominent in my activities. She is assisting me in enhancing my psychic abilities and perception. Our connection allows for the projection of my past appearances, possibly from past lives, into my current videos, adding a profound layer of meaning to these visuals.

Furthermore, I've been exploring the potential to develop these occurrences into a practical skill. This includes understanding messages conveyed through symbols, such as those from Hebrew or Egyptian cultures which are particularly significant to me. Recently, I invoked a meditation to connect with Dominique and successfully saw his image in a video review session.

This breakthrough has excited me about the possibilities of using this ability to seek guidance that aligns with the highest good. However, I am mindful not to misuse this connection for trivial or selfish gains, such as predicting lottery numbers or sports' outcomes, as that would not reflect the true purpose of this spiritual guidance.

These developments mark a new chapter in my spiritual journey, one that deeply connects my past and present, enhancing my understanding of the universe and my role within it.

Since intensifying my spiritual practice around 2016, I've spent eight years on a journey rich with revelations. While we may occasionally feel we've reached a peak, experiencing moments that seem like the ultimate pinnacle of our spiritual quest, the journey is unending. Spiritual growth is a continuous evolution; every advancement discloses new insights and deeper experiences, underscoring that our journey is not about reaching a final destination but evolving and expanding our understanding and connection with the universe. I acknowledge that my own exploration is far from over. Even as I envision my final moments, I anticipate a continued curiosity about the expansive realm of mysticism.

I advocate for a proactive approach to spirituality, where individuals don't just passively accept the idea of guardian angels or spirit guides but actively seek to connect with them. Learning their names, understanding their roles, and interacting with them can enhance your spiritual journey, offering insights and experiences that enrich your lives. This connection is about fostering a relationship that allows for interactive experiences through visions and other spiritual encounters.

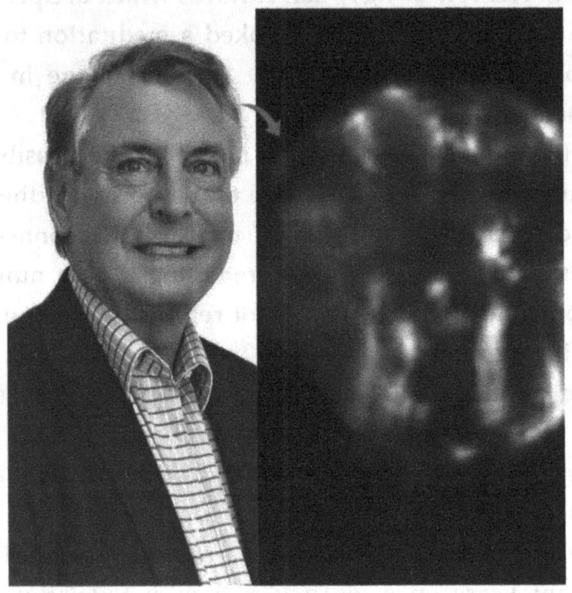

This was a shocker! As I was trying to connect my consciousness to the Holy Ones, my image appeared on the left side of the orb. Is this proof that we can connect our thoughts and emotions to those on the other side or is the message that we are connected to everything and everyone?

In Conclusion

In closing the pages of our journey together through spirituality, we must acknowledge the absolute influence of relationships, not just with fellow humans but with all beings that grace our lives. My own path toward spiritual enlightenment was profoundly shaped by a being of pure love and innocence – my beloved dog, Boo Boo. This journey chronicled within these pages might have taken a different turn, or perhaps not have commenced at all, had it not been for the deep connection and many lessons I learned from my time with her.

Boo Boo taught me about unconditional love, the beauty of living in the moment, and the genuine connections that transcend spoken language, nudging me toward a deeper understanding of the interconnectedness of all life. This unique bond highlighted the essence of spirituality to me: the recognition and celebration of unity and sacredness in all forms of life.

As we part ways through the medium of this book, I invite you to embrace the relationships in your life, both seen and unseen, as catalysts for your spiritual journey. Cherish the silent teachings and the loud lessons they offer. Let the love, the challenges, the joys, and even the sorrows they bring be your guideposts toward deeper introspection and spiritual awakening.

May you carry forward the essence of this journey, integrating the insights and reflections into your everyday life. Let the stories and the wisdom contained in these pages be a lantern on your path, illuminating how you navigate the intricacies of your unique spiritual expedition. Remember, spirituality is not just about seeking – it's about recognizing that which is already present, the divine spark within every moment, every creature, and every interaction.

In honor of Boo Boo and all the beings who guide us, knowingly or unknowingly, on our spiritual path, I bid you farewell on this chapter of your journey, with the hope that it serves as a stepping stone toward your own enlightening adventure.

May your path be blessed with light, love, and the joy of discovery as you unfold the infinite layers of your spiritual essence.

With much gratitude,

Tim

Author Biographies

Tim Malone

Tim Malone is an accomplished entrepreneur with a passion for business innovation. Prior to joining the family business, Malone Workforce Solutions, in 1998, he successfully owned and operated a profitable flooring company. Taking the reins alongside his brothers, Tim has been instrumental in significantly increasing sales from 20 million dollars in revenue to 411 million dollars. All the while spearheading the acquisition or initiation of several other businesses at the same time. Tim firmly believes that exceptional customer service is the cornerstone of Malone's success. His leadership philosophy centers on fostering a collaborative work environment where all employees work together in achieving both business and personal goals.

Tim started his spiritual journey nearly a decade ago, determined to understand the mysteries of the universe. This was an unexpected new chapter in his life, one he expects to keep evolving. *Behind the Veil* is the first of a series of books that Tim plans to write and publish.

Tim is also an avid enthusiast of music, golf, and fishing, and enjoys spending quality time with his family.

Jessica Franzini

Jessica served as the director of public relations for tennis and volleyball events at the Great Western Forum in Los Angeles, the East San Diego County Association of Realtors in San Diego, and The Hay Group in Singapore.

Upon returning to the States, Jessica ventured out on her own to become a one-woman writing company. In addition to her ghostwriting talents, she often serves as a lead communications strategist for companies, producing both their internal and external work product.

Over the past decade, Jessica has become a publishing field expert, guiding clients through the complexities of publishing their own projects. After having served as the editor for numerous published titles, *Behind the Veil* is her first book as a named coauthor.

Jessica is happy to point out that everyone in her family is a professional writer. Her husband Lou, a clinical psychologist, is also the author of five books, and their son, Sam, is a culture writer and novelist, living in Washington, DC. Jessica and Lou now enjoy their empty nest in Jacksonville Beach, Florida, with their rescue pup, Charlie.

Note to Readers

Thank you for purchasing *Behind the Veil: One Man's Journey from Opioid Addiction to Spirituality and Beyond.* It has been an amazing, invigorating, cathartic, and challenging experience to craft my story for your enjoyment, and I am truly grateful you have joined me on this journey. If you have a few moments, please add your review of the book to your favorite online site.

I am more than happy to stay in touch with you! If you have any questions or would like to keep up with what I am doing next, please visit my website at thetimmalone.com.

Recommended Reading

If You Are Just Beginning Your Journey

Birthing a New Civilization: Transition to the New Golden Age in 2032, Diana Cooper
The Secret, Rhonda Byrne
Ask Your Guides, Sonia Choquette
The Orb Project, Miceal Ledwith and Klaus Heinemann
Dying to be Me, Anita Moorjani
Meet Your Guides: Embracing Your Angels, Archangels, and Ascended Masters, Deborah Sudarsky
Lessons from the Light: What We Can Learn from the Near-Death Experience, Kenneth Ring and Evelyn Elsaesser Valarino
The Divine Matrix, Gregg Braden
The Amazing Afterlife of Animals, Karen A. Anderson
Twin Flame Transcendence: The Spiritual Journey of Twin Flames, Emily Jennings
Sea Stories: My Life in Special Operations, William H. McRaven
A Little Light on the Spiritual Laws, Diana Cooper
Ascension Through Orbs, Diana Cooper and Kathy Crosswell
The History of Atlantis, Lewis Spence
The Boy Who Saw True, Anonymous

If You Have Several Years of Experience

Phenomena: Code of the Grand Original Design, Klaus Heinemann, Ph.D. and Gundi Heinemann
Orbs: Their Mission and Messages of Hope, Klaus Heinemann, Ph.D. and Gundi Heinemann
Expanding Perception: Re-discovering the Grand Original Design, Klaus Heinemann, Ph.D. and Gundi Heinemann
Imagine: Adventures of Our Lives' Journey — Who We Are and What Inspired Us, Klaus Heinemann, Ph.D. and Gundi Heinemann
Journey of Souls, Michael Newton, Ph.D.

The Temples of Light, Danielle Rama Hoffman
From Hell to Heaven, Jakob Lorber
Archangels & Ascended Masters, Doreen Virtue, Ph.D.
The Astral Plane, C.W. Leadbeater

If You Consider Yourself a Master

The Urantia Book: Revealing the Mysteries of God, the Universe, World History, Jesus, and Ourselves, multiple authors
Communing with the Divine: A Clairvoyant's Guide to Angels, Archangels, and the Spiritual Hierarchy, Barbara Y. Martin and Dimitri Moraitis
Being the Change: How One Contemporary Person Initiated Extraordinary Positive Changes in the World by Following the Wisdom Teachings with Totality, Klaus Heinemann, Ph.D. and Gundi Heinemann
The Lightworker's Way, Doreen Virtue
Ramtha: The White Book, Ramtha
Edgar Cayce on Angels, Archangels, and the Unseen Forces, Edgar Cayce
The Middle Pillar, Chic Cicero
The Tibetan Book of Living and Dying, Sogyal Rinpoche

References

(No date a) *Twin Flame Transcendence: The Spiritual Journey of Twin Flames*, Jennings, Emily. 9798850918071.

(No date b) *Meet Your Guides: Embracing Your Angels, Archangels, and Ascended Masters* ebook, Sudarsky M.Ed., Deborah.

(No date c) *Twin Flames, crystalinks*. Available at: https://www.crystalinks.com/twin_flames.html (Accessed: 8 January 2024).

Akashic Records for Beginners: Can We Access Our Akashic Records? (no date). *Gaia*. Available at: https://www.gaia.com/article/akashic-records-101-can-we-access-our-akashic-records (Accessed: 12 April 2024).

Anderson, K. (2017). *The Amazing Afterlife of Animals: Messages and Signs from our Pets on the Other Side*. Spokane, Washington: Painted Rain Publishing.

Braden, G. (2010). *The Divine Matrix: Bridging Time, Space, Miracles, and Belief*. Strawberry Hills, NSW: Accessible Publishing.

Byrne, R. (2016). *The Secret*. Hillsboro, OR: Simon & Schuster.

Choquette, S. (2021). *Ask Your Guides: Calling in Your Divine Support System for Help with Everything in Life*. Carlsbad, CA: Hay House, Inc.

Cooper, D. (2014). *Birthing a New Civilization: Transition to the New Golden Age in 2032*. Chicago: Findhorn Press.

Cooper, D. and Crosswell, K. (2009). *Ascension Through Orbs*. Forres: Findhorn Press.

First-ever recording of a dying human brain shows waves similar to memory flashbacks (no date). *School of Medicine University of Louisville*. Available at: https://louisville.edu/medicine/news/first-ever-recording-of-a-dying-human-brain-shows-waves-similar-to-memory-flashbacks (Accessed: 19 February 2024).

Ghosts of the Biltmore House (no date). *Ghosts of the Biltmore House | North Carolina Ghosts*. Available at: https://northcarolinaghosts.com/mountains/biltmore-house-ghosts/ (Accessed: 21 August 2023).

Heinemann, K.W. and Heinemann, G. (2014). *Orbs: Their Mission and Messages of Hope*. Carlsbad, CA: Hay House, Inc.

Martin, B.Y. and Moraitis, D. (2021). *Communing with the Divine: A Clairvoyant's Guide to Angels, Archangels, and the Spiritual Hierarchy*. Encinitas, CA: Spiritual Arts Institute.

Newton, M. (2019). *Journey of Souls: Case Studies of Life Between Lives*. Woodbury, MN: Llewellyn Publications.

Newton's Third Law of Motion (no date). *The Physics Classroom*. Available at: https://www.physicsclassroom.com/class/newtlaws/Lesson-4/Newton-s-Third-Law (Accessed: 2 November 2023).

Oddity of Orbs, The (2021). *Stories in the Cemetery*. Available at: https://storiesinthecemetery.com/2020/03/27/the-oddity-of-orbs/ (Accessed: 5 August 2023).

Our Lady of Fatima Miracle (no date). *Our Lady of Fatima Catholic Church*. Available at: https://fatimachurchabq.org/our-lady-of-fatima-miracle#:~:text=The%20story%20begins%20in%20the,ages%2010%2C%209%20and%207. (Accessed: 15 October 2023).

Poirier-Leroy, O. (2019). How Michael Phelps Used Visualization to Stay Calm Under Pressure. *YourSwimLog.com*. Available at: https://www.yourswimlog.com/michael-phelps-visualization/ (Accessed: 9 February 2024).

Rachel Keene (2023). *RACHEL KEENE | HEALING | THERAPY | TUITION*. Available at: https://www.rachelkeene.co.uk/ (Accessed: 19 September 2023).

Ratusny, D. (2024). How do you manifest? The 3 secrets of manifestation. *Insight Timer Blog*. Available at: https://insighttimer.com/blog/how-to-manifest/ (Accessed: 1 April 2024).

Ring, K. and Valarino, E.E. (2006). *Lessons from the Light: What We Can Learn from the Near-Death Experience*. Needham: Moment Point Press.

Southern Spirit Guide (2024). Available at: https://www.southernspiritguide.org/ (Accessed: 3 August 2023).

Taylor, J. and Taylor, J. (1978). *The Bible*. Rutland, VT: Printed by Fay & Davison.

The Urantia Book: Revealing the Mysteries of God, the Universe, World History, Jesus, and Ourselves (2015). Chicago, IL: Urantia Foundation.

Vadlamani, Sonia *et al.* (2022). What is a lightworker and what do they do exactly? *happiness.com*. Available at: https://www.happiness.com/magazine/inspiration-spirituality/what-is-a-lightworker-and-what-do-they-do-exactly/ (Accessed: 28 December 2023).

Virtue, D. (2008). *The Lightworker's Way: Awakening Your Spiritual Power to Know and Heal*. Carlsbad, CA: Hay House.

What Happens in Our Brain When We Die? (2022). *Neuroscience News*. Available at: https://neurosciencenews.com/brain-death-20092/ (Accessed: 27 February 2024).

Zerwick, P. (2024). What Deathbed Visions Teach Us About Living. *The New York Times*. Available at: https://www.nytimes.com/2024/03/12/magazine/deathbed-visions-research.html (Accessed: 13 March 2024).

O-BOOKS

SPIRITUALITY

O is a symbol of the world, of oneness and unity; this eye represents knowledge and insight. We publish titles on general spirituality and living a spiritual life. We aim to inform and help you on your own journey in this life.
If you have enjoyed this book, why not tell other readers by posting a review on your preferred book site?

Recent bestsellers from O-Books are:

Awakening Child
A journey of inner transformation through teaching your child mindfulness and compassion.
Heather Grace MacKenzie
Paperback: 978-1-78535-408-3 ebook: 978-1-78535-409-0

A Colourful Dose of Optimism
Prescribe your own Happy Colours to Feel Good NOW
Jules Standish
It's time for us to look on the bright side, by boosting our mood and lifting our spirit, both in our interiors, as well as our closet.
Paperback: 978-1-78904-927-5 ebook: 978-1-78904-928-2

Natural Happiness

Use Organic Gardening Skills to Cultivate Yourself

Alan Heeks

Deepen your roots to grow through uncertainty.

Paperback: 978-1-80341-496-6 ebook: 978-1-80341-497-3

Daylight Saving Time

The Power of Growing Older

David W. Berner

Daylight Saving Time: Facing age with grace and mindfulness.

Paperback: 978-1-80341-511-6 ebook: 978-1-80341-520-8

Generation Panic

Simple & Empowering Techniques to Combat Anxiety

Agi Heale

Generation Panic is a one-stop shop with over 100 tips and techniques to help busy professionals combat anxiety.

Paperback: 978-1-78904-515-4 ebook: 978-1-78904-516-1

Life Before the Internet

What we can learn from the good old days

Michael Gentle

A fascinating look back at a slower, simpler time, when Amazon was just a river.

Paperback: 978-1-80341-388-4 ebook: 978-1-80341-389-1

Breath for Health
A Mindful Way to Restore Your Natural Breathing Cycle
Michael D Hutchinson
Discover the secrets hidden in yoga and modern physiology — and restore your natural, healthy, confident way of breathing in just 10 minutes a day.
Paperback: 978-1-80341-440-9 ebook: 978-1-80341-441-6

Readers of ebooks can buy or view any of these bestsellers by clicking on the live link in the title. Most titles are published in paperback and as an ebook. Paperbacks are available in traditional bookshops. Both print and ebook formats are available online.

Find more titles and sign up to our readers' newsletter at
www.o-books.com

Follow O-Books on Facebook at **O-Books**

For video content, author interviews, and more, please subscribe to our YouTube channel:

O-BOOKS Presents

Follow us on social media for book news, promotions, and more:

Facebook: O-Books

Instagram: @o_books_mbs

X: @obooks

Tik Tok: @ObooksMBS

www.o-books.com